A BARTHOLOMEW

WALK SOUTH WALES AND THE WYE VALLEY

40 WALKS SELECTED & DESCRIBED
BY DAVID PERROTT AND LAURENCE MAIN

JOHN BARTHOLOMEW & SON LTD
EDINBURGH

CONTENTS

British Library Cataloguing in Publication Data
Perrott, David
    Walk South Wales and the Wye Valley
    1. South Wales — Visitors' guides 2 England. Wye Valley
    — Visitors' Guides   I. Title II. Main, Laurence
    914.29'404858
    ISBN 0–7028–0904–7

Published and Printed in Scotland by
John Bartholomew & Son Ltd, Duncan Street, Edinburgh EH9 1TA.

First Edition 1989
Copyright © John Bartholomew & Son Ltd, 1989.

ISBN 0 7028 0904 7

Produced for John Bartholomew & Son Ltd by
Perrott Cartographics, Darowen, Machynlleth, Powys SY20 8NS.
Typesetting and litho origination by Litho Link Ltd, Welshpool.

The physical landscape of Britain is changing all the time; eg. as new
tracks are made, hedges grubbed up and fields amalgamated. While
every care has been taken in the preparation of this guide, neither
the authors, Perrott Cartographics nor John Bartholomew & Son
Ltd will be responsible for any loss, damage or inconvenience
caused by inaccuracies.

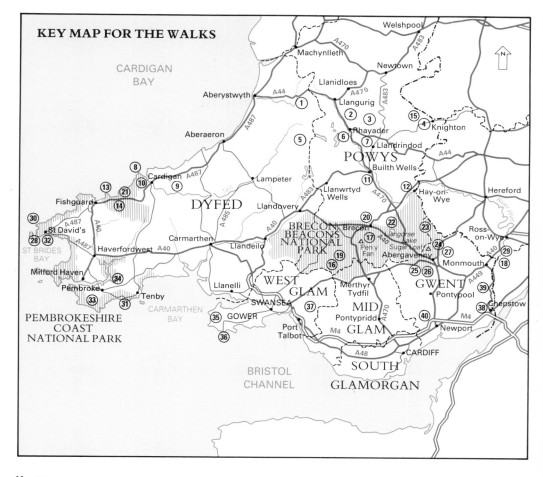

KEY MAP FOR THE WALKS

CARDIGAN BAY

Welshpool

Machynlleth

Newtown

Llanidloes

Aberystwyth

Llangurig

Aberaeron

Rhayader

Knighton

Llandrindod

POWYS

Builth Wells

Cardigan

Lampeter

Llanwrtyd Wells

Hay-on-Wye

Hereford

Fishguard

DYFED

Llandovery

Llandeilo

St David's

Carmarthen

Haverfordwest

ST BRIDES BAY

Ross-on-Wye

Milford Haven

BRECON BEACONS NATIONAL PARK

Brecon

Crickhowell

Sugar Loaf

Abergavenny

Monmouth

Pembroke

Tenby

Llanelli

WEST GLAM

Merthyr Tydfil

GWENT

Pontypool

Chepstow

PEMBROKESHIRE COAST NATIONAL PARK

CARMARTHEN BAY

SWANSEA

GOWER

MID GLAM

Pontypridd

Newport

Port Talbot

GLAM

CARDIFF

BRISTOL CHANNEL

SOUTH GLAMORGAN

Key to maps

Scale 1:63360

0   1 mile

0   1 km

Scale 1:25000

0   1 mile

0   1 km

All maps are drawn on a north axis, ie. with north at the top

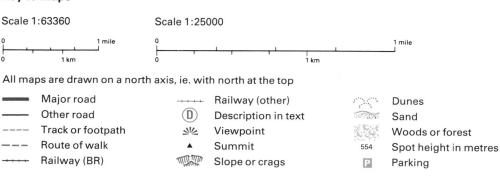

▬▬	Major road	+++	Railway (other)	⠂⠂	Dunes
───	Other road	Ⓓ	Description in text		Sand
----	Track or footpath	⬗	Viewpoint		Woods or forest
---	Route of walk	▲	Summit	554	Spot height in metres
+++	Railway (BR)		Slope or crags	Ⓟ	Parking

3

Walking in South Wales and the Wye Valley

South Wales contains two of the 10 national parks in England and Wales: the Pembrokeshire Coast, which is the smallest with an area of 225 square miles (582 km²), and the Brecon Beacons, which has an area of 519 square miles (1334 sq km) and was the last to be designated, in 1957. This is a tribute to the rugged beauty of an area which is only one-tenth the size of England. Pembrokeshire is the 'Gwlad hud a lledrith' or Land of Mystery and Magic of the 'Mabinogion', the book of Welsh stories written in the 14th century. This special character reflects the unimaginable age of the contorted rocks which create such a dramatic landscape. The spectacular coastline is warmed by the Gulf Stream, while a visit in the spring or early summer brings a bonus of being able to walk on a carpet of wildflowers. Inland, the high moorland and jagged peaks of the Preseli Hills mark a place of great mystic significance, the source of the bluestones erected at Stonehenge.

Few people thought of South Wales as a tourist attraction in the early 20th century. Its image then was of mining valleys, coal trains and steelworks. Incredibly, that world has disappeared. Pits have been turned into heritage centres and the natural beauty of the area, much of which remained unspoiled, has been enhanced by those industrial relics which still remain. Its proximity to Swansea didn't stop the Gower Peninsula becoming Britain's first Area of Outstanding Natural Beauty, while the splendour of the Brecon Beacons was long known to the people of the valleys. Unlike Snowdonia, these mountains are rounded, smooth in outline and with gradual gradients (excluding a steep, northern scarp slope), but these harmonious vistas can be deceptively dangerous. It's an easy climb on a fine day in summer to the 2907 ft (886 m) summit of Pen y Fan, but it can be less friendly in winter or in bad weather. South of here outcrops of limestone which underlie the coal measures form the 'Waterfall Country' around Ystradfellte.

The Wye rises near the Severn on the slopes of Pumlumon Fawr but the two rivers don't meet until they are south of Chepstow. The Welsh heartland provides tourists with delightful surprises as the Wye races towards the English border at Hay. A brief flirtation with Herefordshire is ended near Symond's Yat. From here, the river flows close to the border, being overlooked by Offa's Dyke. The wonderful scenery is that which the cult followers of the 'picturesque' flocked to admire in the 18th century. What's more, the Wye's freedom from pollution has conserved a particularly wide range of plant and animal life.

1 SAFETY FIRST

The walks in this guide are intended for the enjoyment of all, including those with no prior experience and who possess a minimum of equipment, and are quite safe if approached with common sense. Even our suggested mountain walks are not too strenuous but, before undertaking these, there are simple precautions you must take. The best part of climbing a mountain is to enjoy the view from the top, so if the weather isn't fine, don't go. Always remember that there is the potential danger of a sudden change in the weather and be prepared for this. The climb to the top of Pen y Fan, for example, means a 9°F (5°C) drop in temperature (without allowing for the windchill factor). You can easily get lost in the mist on top of a mountain when the valley is warm and sunny. Avoid venturing on the higher walks alone until you've gained experience of bad weather conditions. All of the high mountain walks in this guide have been deliberately planned as there-and-back routes, so note landmarks when ascending so that you can find your way down easily.

Good, sound equipment is essential for these high level walks. Walking boots or stout walking shoes are the most important item - don't rely on training shoes, wellington boots or sandals. Several layers of clothing are preferable to one heavy jersey. Avoid jeans (which are very uncomfortable if soaked) and carry a pair of trousers (tracksuit trousers are ideal) if you're wearing shorts. After boots, an anorak with a hood is the next most important item. It should keep out the wind and be waterproof. A warm hat and gloves are also recommended. Always carry some spare emergency clothing, plus a torch and batteries. Food and drink are other vital items. Make sure you have plenty.

A 1:25 000 scale map is essential for high mountain walks, especially Pen y Fan. Practise relating your route to the map and be able to give a grid reference in case you have to fetch help for a friend. If you are caught in mist, a good compass is reliable - your own sense of direction is not. Practise using a map and compass in easy conditions before you have to rely on them when things are difficult.

Plan your walk allowing plenty of time to complete it, including having a picnic and enjoying the views. Notice bad weather escape routes. Tell someone where you're going and when you should be back. Regrettably, a spate of thefts from walkers' cars means that it may no longer be wise to write where you're going on a note displayed inside the windscreen of your car. Remember that heavy rain can make streams impassable. Don't attempt to cross such streams in spate. If in doubt, turn back. Avoid jumping dangerously from boulder to boulder. Take particular care in the 'Waterfall Country' of Ystradfellte, where delighted children will need to be watched closely. Perhaps the most dangerous places, especially for unsupervised children, are the cliffs of the Pembrokeshire Coast Path. *Take extra care here and don't let the young ones dash ahead.*

Walk with a steady rhythm. Look to place your feet on level ground and let the whole of the foot contact the ground, not just the toe. Wear only what is necessary, but do stop to put on extra clothing as required. Take short steps on uneven ground and take care not to dislodge loose stones onto walkers below. If in a party, walk to the pace of the slowest member and keep the party together but in single file. Appoint a 'rear person' to ensure no one is left behind. Don't overtake the leader but do take note of your route so that you could lead if necessary. Remember to carry a whistle for emergency distress signals (and use a torch in the dark). Note where the nearest telephone is should you need to make a 999 call and always have some 10p coins available in case you get stranded and need to telephone a friend. Practise on easy walks such as Llyn Syfaddan and Carew before tackling the mountains.

2 RIGHTS OF WAY

Keep to the paths, whether a long established right of way or a courtesy path. The national parks do not have freedom of access, and even on the central area of the Brecon Beacons, which is owned by the National Trust, farmers have grazing rights. If you have a dog, please remember to leave it behind if you are likely to encounter sheep. The Animals Act (1971) states that dogs endangering livestock may be shot. The Protection of Livestock Act (1953) makes it an offence to permit a dog to worry livestock, with a maximum penalty of 200. Worrying includes being at large in a field in which there are sheep. Always regard it as a privilege to follow a path across someone else's land; in that way we can build an atmosphere of co-operation, rather than confrontation, in the countryside.

County Councils, as highway authorities, hold and maintain the definitive maps and statements that are legal proofs of public rights of way. Unfortunately many paths are obstructed and, as a result, neglected. The routes in this guide have been chosen for their lack of obstructions. County Councils have been asked to bring some of the walks up to the required standard by erecting stiles over fences and placing metal signposts where the paths leave roads. Further information on rights of way is available from the Ramblers' Association, 1-5 Wandsworth Road, London, SW8 2LJ.

3 THE COUNTRY CODE

Enjoy the countryside and respect its life and work.
Guard against all risk of fire.
Leave gates as you find them.
Keep your dogs under close control.
Keep to public paths across farmland.
Use gates and stiles to cross fences, hedges and walls.
Leave livestock, crops and machinery alone.
Take your litter home.
Help to keep all water clean.
Protect wildlife, plants and trees.
Take special care on country roads.
Make no unnecessary noise.

4 WELSH HISTORY

Welsh history can be said to begin with the hunter from Palaeolithic times (Old Stone Age) whose skeleton was found in the Paviland Caves in Gower. Maybe the blood of this member of the Cro-Magnon race has managed to survive but it must be well diluted with that of the short, dark people who came from Iberia in the Neolithic (New Stone) Age and by the Celts who came from Central Europe in the Iron Age, speaking Brythonic, from which modern Welsh is descended. When the Romans invaded they found the Silures of South Wales, led by Caradog, their toughest opponents. It was from the royal family of Caradog that King Arthur emerged to rally the Britons when the Romans had departed and Britain was being invaded by Saxons. Arthur ruled alongside his father Meurig, son of Tewdrig, in a territory which covered the modern Glamorgans, Gwent and included parts of what are now the English counties of Gloucestershire and Somerset, including Glastonbury. His base was at Cerniw in Gwent and he was active in the sixth century. Arthur's victories halted the Saxon advance and ensured the survival of the culture and language of the original Britons to the present day. The reality of the border was confirmed when King Offa of the Mercians built his Dyke in the eighth century.

The wide coastal plain of South Wales proved inviting to invaders from England, however. Alfred the Great worked for a client state in South Wales and it was the western kingdom of Deheubarth, the modern Dyfed, which produced Hywel Dda. He came to rule all of Wales except the south-east, issuing his own coinage and codifying Welsh law before his death in 950. Disunity followed and the principle of English overlordship was generally accepted by 1063, when earl Harold of Wessex made the Welsh princes swear fealty to Edward the Confessor.

It was the Norman victors of the Battle of Hastings who made the chief impact on South Wales, however. In a series of isolated invasions, Norman lords with private armies seized parts of Wales for themselves. Chepstow was the first Norman castle to be established on Welsh soil and all seemed lost when Henry I built his first royal castle at Carmarthen. However, Henry's death in 1135 brought civil war in England and rebellion in Wales. The Normans retained the south-east while the north and west, including Dyfed (except for the region around Pembroke), were able to postpone the loss of their independence for well over a century. When Owain Glyndŵr led the last patriotic fight,

the South Walians were his most lukewarm supporters, but his vision of a tripartite division of Britain, with Wales recovering its 'lost territories' paved the way for the Welsh conquest of Britain under Henry Tudor, who had landed at Milford Haven in 1485. His son, Henry VIII, united Wales with England and started the long and insidious process of anglicization. For all that South Wales has taken the practical view of its place within Britain, its distinct nationality is still very evident.

5 THE MABINOGION

The Mabinogion is the title given to Lady Charlotte Guest's translations from the Red Book of Hergest. This and the White book of Rhydderch preserve 11 prose stories written down in the 14th century. All are uniquely Welsh tales and great literature. They are derived from ancient material kept alive until the time they were written down. Modern English translations are now widely available.

6 NATURAL HISTORY

Pembrokeshire is renowned for its birdlife - peregrine falcons, razorbills and choughs are a few of the species which thrive here. Inland, the deciduous forest that would have reached up to 2000 ft (600 m) has largely disappeared, having often been replaced by conifer plantations. Grassland, acid moor, heather and heath predominate in the Brecon Beacons, but rare arctic-alpine plants also survive here. The best places to see the native deciduous trees are in the 'Waterfall Country' and in the Wye Valley, which is particularly enriched by the wildwood. Here you can see woodpeckers attending to old, rotten trees which in April are surrounded by bluebells, wild garlic and early purple orchids.

7 WELSH LANGUAGE

Welsh national consciousness is symbolised by the Welsh language. Welsh is one of Europe's oldest living languages and is a link with the 6th-century bard Taliesin and the original Britons. It is very similar to the Breton of Brittany, where many Britons settled following the demise of the Roman Empire. Expect to hear Welsh spoken in Dyfed, except for the area known as 'Little England Beyond Wales' in the south of Pembrokeshire. The language survives in the other counties too, especially in the most rural parts of Powys and it's always worth greeting people in Welsh. Even in the so-called anglicised areas, you may see a local's eyes light up and receive a reply in the old tongue. Whilst visitors would not reasonably be expected to learn more than a few courtesies, some outline knowledge of pronunciation will enable you to at least master the place names, which can appear quite daunting to the uninitiated.

Pronunciation – the major points

c – as in cat (never as in century).
ch – as in Scottish loch (never as in chimney).
dd – as in the.
f – as in off.
ll – does not occur in English, but is close to the chl in Lochlane, but aspirated and with emphasis on the l.
r – as in rat and usually 'rolled'.
rh – does not occur in English. The difference between r and rh is similar to that between w and wh as in went and when.
s – as in simple (never as in rose).
th – as in think (never as in the).

Courtesy phrases

Good morning – Bore da (bor-eh-da)
Good afternoon – Prynhawn da (Pre-noun-da)
Good evening – Noswaith dda (Noss-wa-eeth-tha)
It's a fine day – Mae hi'n braf heddiw (My-heen-brav-heth-you)
It's raining again! – Mae hi'n bwrw glaw eto! (My-heen-booroo-glaoo-eh-toe)
It's cold today – Mae hi'n oer heddiw (My-heen-oyer-heth-you)
Please – Os gwelwch yn dda (Oss-gwe-loo-kin-tha)
Thank you very much – Diolch yn fawr (Dee-olc-hen-vawr)
Goodbye – Da boch chi (Da-bok-hee)
Goodnight – Nos da (Noss-da)
And when confronted with a boisterous Welsh-speaking sheep dog: Stop! – Paid! (Pie-d)
Go away! – Cer i ffwrdd (Ker-ee-ffor-th)

8 USEFUL ADDRESSES

The most relevant local Weathercall telephone forecast is on (0898) 500414. This covers all of Dyfed and Powys, which includes all of the Pembrokeshire Coast and most of the Brecon Beacons.

Car parking information is given at the start of each walk, and it is also possible to reach the start of many by public transport. British Rail's scenic Heart of Wales line is useful, while a detailed public transport map can be obtained from Dyfed County Council, Highways & Transportation Dept, Llanstephan Road, Carmarthen, SA31 3LZ. Powys is less well-served by buses but you can telephone (059 787) 207 for details of Crossgates Motor's services, (0982) 552597 for details of Roy Brown's Coaches' services and (0685) 82406 for details of Silverline's services across the Brecon Beacons. Telephone (0222) 371331 for details of the Trawscambria bus services.

Public transport is less of a problem in the more densely populated counties of Glamorgan (now divided into South, Mid and West) and Gwent. Roverbus tickets which offer excellent value can be bought. Telephone (0792) 475511 for the Swansea area, (0222) 371331 for the Cardiff area and (029 12) 2947 for the Wye Valley.

Wales Tourist Board
P.O. Box 1, Cardiff, CF1 2XN. Tel: (0222) 27281.

Mid Wales Tourism Council
Canolfan Owain Glyndŵr, Machynlleth, Powys, SY20 8EE. Tel: (0654) 2401.

Brecon Beacons National Park
7 Glamorgan Street, Brecon, Powys, LD3 7DP. Tel: (0874) 4437.

Pembrokeshire Coast National Park
County Offices, Haverfordwest, Dyfed, SA61 1QZ. Tel: (0437) 4591.

Offa's Dyke Association
Old Primary School, West Street, Knighton, Powys. Tel: (0547) 528753.

Walk 1
PONTARFYNACH (DEVIL'S BRIDGE)
7 miles (11.2 km) Moderate

Cwm Rheidol must rank as one of the most attractive valleys in Wales, with native oak forests surviving to clothe the valley sides. The walker will also see fine views and waterfalls, while the start of this walk can be approached in style (during the summer) aboard a steam-hauled train from Aberystwyth. Arrive on the first train and leave on the last, to allow at least four hours for this walk.

A The Vale of Rheidol Railway was opened in 1902 to serve the needs of both Vale of Rheidol lead mines and tourists. It has a gauge of 1 ft 11 ins (0.59 m approx) and a gradient of 1 in 48 over the 12 miles (19.2 km) from Aberystwyth to Devil's Bridge. At first the line carried huge quantities of ore but this traffic had virtually ceased by 1913 when the Cambrian Railways took over the line. Local goods traffic continued until 1927 but the Great Western Railway, who took over the line in 1922, invested in new engines and carriages for the tourist traffic. Their 'Owain Glyndŵr' and 'Llywelyn' survive today, as does the original company's 'Prince of Wales' (which the G.W.R. rebuilt).

Attempts were made to close the line in 1954 and in 1963 but it proved too popular, attracting as many as 180,000 tourists in 1975. Offered for sale by British Rail in 1988, an active Supporters' Association exists to see it thrive in the future. The return train journey allows you to relive the walk, which is located between Devil's Bridge and Rheidol Falls.

B Rheidol Falls has a fish ladder to help fish overcome this height. A hydro-electric power station lies down river. Turn left down the road after the falls if you'd like to visit the Central Electricity Generating Board Reception Centre.

C Castell Bwa-drain is an old hill-fort with fine views

D The waterfall in Nant Bwa-drain can be seen from the train across the valley.

E Native sessile oak forest, the natural climax vegetation for the major part of Wales under 2,000 ft (609 m). Over-grazing by sheep and the planting of conifers have now made such glorious forests rare.

F Cwm Rheidol lead mine, from which an aerial ropeway ran to the railway across the valley. The filter beds near the footbridge (Pontbren Plwca) precipitate lead out of the stream before it is used in the Rheidol power station, to avoid killing the fish.

G On your return continue past the railway station for 300 yds (270 m) to the modern road bridge that covers two older bridges across the Afon Mynach. To see the oldest bridge, you'll have to put a coin in a slot (1 in 1988, plus 50p to visit the Devil's Punch Bowl). The oldest bridge, at the bottom, is said to date from 1087 and to have been built by monks from Strata Florida (Afon Mynach means Monk's River). As this was nearly a century before the monks built the abbey, the claim must be doubted. The middle bridge was built about 1708.

The top, iron bridge dates from the 20th century, so George Borrow didn't see it when he came this way, describing his journey in his book *Wild Wales*, (1862). Your money does also provide access to a fine nature trail and a spectacular gorge, with a splendid view of the Afon Mynach as it cascades down a 'hanging valley' to join the Rheidol. The Rheidol turned south to join the Afon Teifi until its present upper section was captured by the headwaters of the lower Rheidol cutting back into the hills. No wonder the Rheidol's energy has been tapped to produce electricity! According to legend, the first bridge was built by the devil so that an old lady could retrieve a stray cow. Payment was to be the first living thing that crossed it. The old lady outwitted the devil by enticing her dog across first with a crust of bread. The devil had the dog and the old lady her cow.

PONTARFYNACH (DEVIL'S BRIDGE)
Continued

0   1 mile

0   1 km

5 *Turn right, through a gate, to walk with the fence on your left down to a stream. Continue past a ruin, veer right to the fence for a view of the waterfall and the valley.*

6 *When the fence swings left, cross a stile to zig-zag down through the oak trees until another path cuts across yours just above a stile. Turn left along this path. When you reach a stream, ignore the stile on your right but cross the stream just above the fence, turn right through a gate and follow a fence round on your left to an uphill path. Veer right, with the fence, after a gate.*

7 *Cross a stile before a stream to follow a track downhill, with conifers on your left. Veer right at a fork downhill to a road. Turn right to a signpost where you turn left over a footbridge. Turn left after a gate uphill, cross a stile on your left to follow the path to no 2 and back to the start.*

1 *Park your car at Devil's Bridge station (small fee). This is on the A4120, about 12 miles (19.2 m) east of Aberystwyth. Turn right along this road from the station until the gate just after the last bungalow on your right, where an old sign points to Cwm Rheidol and Ystumtuen. Go ahead across the field and turn left at the top of the gorge. Walk with the wooded slopes on your right until you cross a stile ahead of you, near the railway. Walk to a gate on your right and cross the railway carefully to a woodland path which leads back to the railway at a stile. Keep the railway on your left as you walk carefully beside it for 100 yds (90 m) before turning right at the stump of an old stile and down wooden steps. Bear left downhill through a conifer forest, keeping left at a forest track. Follow an open hillside path to a fork.*

Bwa-drain

Nant Bwa-drain

C

Cwm Rheidol

D

B

Ty-poeth

E

Coed Simdde-lwyd

Afon Rheidol

F

4 *Walk past Typoeth to a stile in a fence ahead of you. Walk uphill, forking right into the trees after a small gate. Turn right when you reach conifers until a stile on the left leads to an uphill path through these trees. Cross a stile back into oak forest and walk up to bare hillside. Walk ahead, away from the valley and with an old hill-fort on your left. Pass a ruin on your right and walk towards the stream. Turn left along a track to cross the stream and walk up to a lane. Turn right, passing an old waterwheel on your right, until just before the lane bends left.*

Vale of Rheidol Railway

A

3 *Go ahead with the forest on your left and the river across a field on your right. When the path forks, keep to the lower, right, path, at the foot of the forest. Cross a stream carefully and pass old mine ruins on your right. Bear right towards the river and cross a stile to follow a fenced path past the Rheidol Falls. Turn right over the footbridge and walk to a road where you turn right for 150 yds (137 m). Turn left up a track.*

To Aberystwyth
A4120

Pontarfynach
(Devil's Bridge)

G

2 *Follow the higher path, on your left, at the fork. Walk through oak trees to reach a fence on your right. When the track forks near the river, keep on the upper, left, track, at the foot of the forest.*

Walk 2
PONT MARTEG
11 miles (17.6 km) Moderate

This is a glorious walk. Don't be put off by its length. It is mostly over clear tracks, probably as ancient as the standing stones that can be seen along the way. You reach an altitude of 1600 feet (488 m), but the ascent is very gradual and this is a moorland plateau walk, rather than a mountain climb. Nevertheless, use a map and compass to make sure you don't miss the road! The 'Powys Beast' (see below) has been seen in this area recently, thus adding mystery to the beautiful scenery.

A Pont Marteg is the bridge over the Afon Marteg, a tributary of the Wye, above the confluence of the two rivers. Trains of the Mid Wales Railway used to steam past here but now there is a popular picnic site for weary motorists. A lady from Chester stopped here in the late spring of 1980. To her amazement she saw a 'puma' sunning itself on the rocks. Then a second, smaller creature, resembling a lynx, appeared. In October 1980, a nearby farmer, Michael Nash of Pant-y-drain, between Pont Marteg and Llangurig, found carcases of four sheep which had obviously been eaten. Other carcases were found, a woman saw a cat-like animal and strange snoring sounds were heard from a haybarn. Four inch (10 cm) cat-like prints were found in mud outside the barn. RSPCA Inspector Trevor Caldwell was called in on 24th October, 1980, but the 'cat' had slipped away by the time police marksmen surrounded the barn and helicopters hovered overhead. A thorough search of the barn found straw that stank 'like a big cat's house in a zoo', according to Sgt Ken Davies. More sightings of the 'Powys Beast' followed and the police took more casts of prints which were the size of a small palm, with claws about the size of a finger. A Powys County Council

surveyor spotted a tawny-coloured 'puma' further north, near Staylittle and, on 11th May, 1981, a large 'cat' killed 7 ewes and 5 lambs at Ysbyty Ystwyth. Sightings are still recorded. A taxi-driver reported a 'lion' near Aberystwyth in March 1982, while a 'panther' was seen near Cwmystwyth in September 1985. There are plenty of hiding-places in old mine shafts and quarries in this wild area. Rest assured that it has never attacked a human.

B Maengwyngweddw is a conspicuous boulder of white quartz that stands 3 feet (0.9 m) high and has a circumference of 6 ft 8 ins (2 m).

C Clap-yr-arian was where two cairns stood until October 1910, when Rhayader District Council destroyed the larger one and carted away its stones for road metal. Its foundation layer shows a circumference of about 156 ft (46.8 m). A perfect specimen of a battle-axe came from it, made out of spotted blue dolerite from Preseli. The occupant of this grave may even have helped transport the 'bluestones' to Stonehenge. Bronze Age Beaker People probably established these ridgeway routes when they came here in about 2000 B.C, and the moors are littered with

many of their monuments.

D Maen serth is a prominent standing stone which stands 7 ft 2 ins (2.1 m) high, 6 ins (0.15 m) thick and 1 ft 8 ins (0.5 m) broad, at an altitude of 1500 ft (460 m). It is thought to be of Bronze Age origin, despite the tradition that it marks the spot where Einion Clud, the Welsh chieftain of Elvel, was murdered by the English after he had unhorsed Roger Mortimer in a tournament in the late 12th century. This story may well explain the deeply incised cross with 5 inch (0.13 m) long arms, on the side facing east-south-east.

0 _____ 1 mile
0 _____ 1 km

1 Park your car at Pont Marteg, where there is a picnic area. This is at the side of a minor road which meets the A470 where the signpost says 'St Harmon 2' and will be found 3 miles (4.8 km) north of Rhayader, where the A44 meets the A470. Walk back to the A470 and cross it, bearing right to a footbridge over the River Wye. Turn right after crossing this bridge and follow the Wye upstream, crossing a fence where there are the remains of a stile. Climb very gradually uphill on your left to pass through a gap in the old wall ahead. Pass a large, isolated rock on your right and continue to an old gate in the fence ahead. Keep on this path, very gradually bearing left uphill until you reach a lane. Remember where you join this lane for your return journey!

2 Turn left along the lane and walk above the large, isolated rock you passed earlier. REMEMBER IT AS A GOOD LANDMARK FOR YOUR RETURN JOURNEY. Continue with the fence on your left, go through a gate ahead and bend right with the lane. Just before a house on your left, turn right along a signposted bridleway.

3 After climbing with the bridleway to go through a gate, turn left over the low fence and walk uphill to rejoin the track at a gate in the fence ahead. Go through this gate and bear slightly right uphill to a small gate in the fence ahead. Turn right uphill, then bear left slightly along an obvious track. Keep left at a fork.

4 Ford a stream and continue, to reach a quiet mountain road. Turn left along this road. Notice a track leaving the road on your left. Continue along the road to a lay-by on your right. Bear left away from the road here, soon joining the track passed previously. Go ahead along this track, passing a white, quartz stone on your left (Maengwyngweddw). The track bears a little to the right shortly after this.

5 A track joins yours from the right. About a quarter of a mile (0.4 km) after this, notice a standing stone (Maen serth) about 50 yds (45 m) away on your left. Return to the clear track after visiting the standing stone. Continue along it, eventually walking past conifer trees on your left. When another track meets yours from the right, bear left along the grass with the fence on your left. When the fence bends left, swing right along the green track to rejoin the stony track. Turn left downhill with the fence on your right.

6 Go through a gate and turn left along a lane. The River Wye and the trackbed of the dismantled Mid Wales Railway are down on your right. Remember to look out for the large, isolated rock you passed on the outward journey. Continue along the lane to point **2**, where you turn right to retrace your steps to the start.

11

ABATY CWMHIR (ABBEYCWMHIR)
4.5 miles (7.2) km Easy

Abbeycwmhir, or 'the abbey of the long valley', is one of the chief attractions of the 'Glyndŵr's Way' long distance path. Although there is little in the way of ruins, there is enough to show the enormous length of the nave. Students of Welsh independence can make a pilgrimage to a modern slate slab which commemorates Llywelyn ap Gruffydd (the Last), whose headless body was taken here for burial after he had died in a skirmish near Builth Wells in 1282. The English had cut off his head to exhibit it in London. This walk follows a short section of 'Glyndŵr's Way' which was an ancient pathway called the Monk's Way since it linked Abbeycwmhir with the abbey at Strata Florida. Your path then goes through the conifers of the Forestry Commission. There are fine views, a stretch of open country, some broadleaved trees and interesting streams. The paths are good and the 'Happy Union Inn' awaits your return.

A Abbeycwmhir is a remote spot enclosed by magnificent hills. This situation attracted the Cistercians, an order of monks founded at Citeaux in France by St Robert of Molesmes in 1098. Abbeycwmhir was founded in 1143 by Maredudd ap Iorwerth. The original site was at Ty-faenor, about one mile (1.6 km) east of here. The Anglo-Norman conquest of Maredudd's lordship of Maelienydd in 1144 probably caused this to be a short-lived venture, however. The abbey was refounded at its present site in 1176 by Cadwallon ap Madoc, the new lord of Maelienydd and a cousin of Rhys ap Gruffydd, prince of South Wales. It was a daughter house of Whitland, the abbey in Dyfed founded by Rhys ap Gruffydd. The Norman Marcher lords Roger Mortimer and William Fitzalan may even have set aside their differences with the Welsh to help found Abbeycwmhir. Certainly the abbey was to be treated with suspicion by both sides in subsequent wars and meant that the building of the abbey was never to be completed. From its plan, however, it would have become one of the largest in Britain, after Winchester, York and Durham. The manor house at Ty-faenor was to be built with stones plundered from the ruins of the dissolved abbey in the early 17th century.

The Cistercians chose solitude to encourage self-sufficiency and the abbey had its own mill, well and bakehouse. The Clywedog Brook was used to provide water-power, while its fish would have been an important part of the diet of the monks, who originally abstained from eating flesh. They kept sheep, however, chopping down the native deciduous forests for grazing land. By the end of the 12th century, Abbeycwmhir had itself founded a daughter house at Cymer, near Dolgellau (Gwynedd). 1231 saw the abbey involved in the politics that were to stunt its growth. Llywelyn ab Iorwerth (Llywelyn the Great) persuaded an abbot to give false information to Henry III's men which led to them being slaughtered. Perhaps the good abbot was misled by the crafty Llewelyn. Henry III plundered Abbeycwmhir in revenge and the abbey itself was only saved from destruction by the payment of 300 marks to the King. The abbey's Welsh national sentiments, and not just its location near Builth Wells (where llywelyn died), must have led to Llywelyn the Last's headless body being buried here in 1282. Owain Glyndŵr sacked and destroyed the abbey in 1401, however, since he suspected its monks were English spies. The abbey was under the patronage of the Mortimers and Glyndŵr adopted a scorched earth policy against them. There were only three monks in residence when the abbey was dissolved in 1536. Turned into a Royalist fort in the Civil War, it was stormed by the Roundheads in 1644. The ruins were used as a quarry right up to the rebuilding of the parish church in 1866 and the building of the Hall in 1869.

B 'Glyndŵr's Way' is a 120 mile long distance path from Knighton to Welshpool via Machynlleth.

0   1 mile

0   1 km

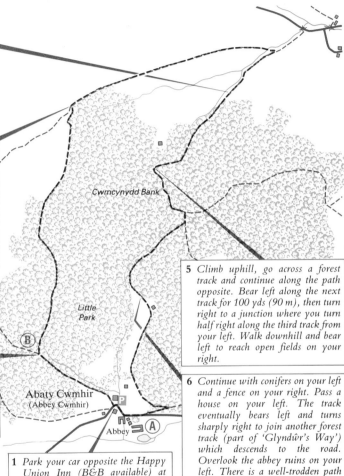

4 *Join a forest track coming from your left and go ahead to join a second forest track also coming from your left. Keep going ahead, soon bearing right. Turn left up a narrow forest path just before the track bends sharply right and crosses a stream.*

3 *Turn right to walk with a fence on your right. Continue through four gates. Follow the path as it crosses a stream on your right to turn sharply right and walk upstream with a fence on your left. Go through a gate and keep beside the stream but do not cross it when you see a gate ahead. Instead, fork left with the stream still on your right. Go through a gate back into the forest.*

2 *Fork right, leaving 'Glyndŵr's Way'. You can hear a stream down on your right, while a track soon joins yours from the left. Maintain your direction straight across another track (i.e. go ahead on the second track from your left) at a junction. Pass a disused quarry on your right. Continue with a clear view on your left and conifers on your right. Ignore forest tracks on your right and bear left over a cattle grid.*

5 *Climb uphill, go across a forest track and continue along the path opposite. Bear left along the next track for 100 yds (90 m), then turn right to a junction where you turn half right along the third track from your left. Walk downhill and bear left to reach open fields on your right.*

6 *Continue with conifers on your left and a fence on your right. Pass a house on your left. The track eventually bears left and turns sharply right to join another forest track (part of 'Glyndŵr's Way') which descends to the road. Overlook the abbey ruins on your left. There is a well-trodden path down to the abbey through a gate on your left. The car park is a few yards along the road, around the bend.*

1 *Park your car opposite the Happy Union Inn (B&B available) at Abbeycwmhir, which is on a minor road about 6 miles (9.6 km) east of Rhayader (please avoid church service times). With your back to the church, turn right and right again up the signposted 'Glyndŵr's Way'. Cross a stile beside a gate and keep to the right hand side of the field. Go through a gate into a conifer forest. Keep straight ahead, ignoring a path looping around to your right.*

Walk 4
TREF-Y-CLAWDD (KNIGHTON)
5 miles (8 km) Moderate

Offa's Dyke was constructed to mark the border between Wales and the old English kingdom of Mercia, so a walk along it involves a foray into England. These days you will not, of course, incur any penalties, although in Offa's day you would have qualified for safe conduct back to Wales by a guide. A climb of 600 ft (180 m) from the floor of the Teme valley is rewarded by fine views across it, into Wales.

A You are advised to visit the Offa's Dyke Heritage Centre Exhibition before examining at first hand this great earthwork, which was built on the order of Offa, king of the Mercians from 757 to 796 AD. It was probably prompted by an unsuccessful Welsh attack in 784. This would have annoyed Offa, who was concentrating his energies on becoming the first king of the English. The Dyke marked an agreed frontier and controlled trade by directing it through defined routeways. It was probably patrolled rather than manned, but it may have had a more than incidental defensive purpose. It is sited on west facing slopes, giving an advantage to Mercian defenders, with the ditch (which is dug on a massive scale in places) practically always facing the Welsh side. The rampart may have had a timber palisade on top. It is likely that Offa never lived to see its construction completed. Like the infamous 'Maginot Line' in France, it had its weak link - a gap in the north where the Welsh still hoped to regain Chester. Agreed laws on such things as cattle-rustling across the Dyke Provide evidence of the stability of most of the border. The Mercians have been identified as the Vandals, who came here from North Africa.

B The short signposted diversion near the start of this walk is to view a fine section of Offa's Dyke and to see the 'Commemoration Stone' where the Offa's Dyke Path was officially opened on 10th July, 1971, by Lord Hunt. This open-air ceremony was preceded by an inaugural walk along part of the path north of Knighton over Panpunton Hill, which is where our walk takes you. The 'Offa's Dyke Path' runs for some 168 miles (269 km) from Chepstow to Prestatyn.

C The right of way follows Offa's Dyke over Panpunton Hill, which affords fine views across the Teme valley, with the wooded knoll of Cnwclas Castle (see Walk 15) visible. The convenient bench was placed here in memory of the late Frank Noble, the founder of the Offa's Dyke Association.

D Kinsley Wood is on the English side of the River Teme, overlooking the Welsh town of Knighton. Different species of trees were planted to depict the letters 'E.R.' in commemoration of the crowning of Queen Elizabeth II.

E Knighton is generally taken to be the English name for the Welsh town of Tref-y-Clawdd (shortened by British Rail to Trefyclo - the bilingual station name is in England, as it happens). A popular theory is that Knighton refers to armed retainers or knights. However, Knighton may be derived from the original Welsh name for this place. This was Cnwc-din, the fort on the hillspur, occupied by the Ancient Britons. Ironically, the current Welsh name refers to an English intrusion with Tref-y-Clawdd meaning 'the town on the dyke'. Its position has brought it fame in the walking world, being the central place on the 'Offa's Dyke Path' and the starting-point for 'Glyndŵr's Way'. In the past, its importance was military. Rhodri Mawr, who was one of only two kings to ever unify Wales, may have fortified the ancient Bryn-y-castell site on the east side of town in about 840. The Norman Mortimers built a stone castle on the west side of town. It was destroyed by Llewellyn ap Gruffydd in 1262, restored by the Mortimers and destroyed again by Owain Glyndŵr in 1402, on his way to the nearby Battle of Pilleth. Its High Street is also known as the 'Narrows' and is said to date from Tudor times. At its foot, near a clock tower, a weekly market is held on Thursdays.

TREF-Y-CLAWDD (KNIGHTON)
Continued

0   1 mile

0   1 km

4 *Turn right along this cart track. Go through a gate and pass trees on your left. Follow a fence on your right until it veers right with a plantation of trees. Strike ahead across the field to the far corner, below the farmhouse on your left.*

3 *Walk along this ridge path at a height of about 1100 ft (335 m), with the fence on your right. Enjoy the fine view over the Teme valley on your left from the Frank Noble Memorial Seat beside the memorial cairn to Roy Waters. Cross several stiles as you walk actually on top of the Dyke, passing a patch of fir trees on your right. Pass farm buildings on your left and continue to a cart track on your right.*

2 *Turn left to walk with the River Teme on your right until you reach a footbridge across the river, immediately before a railway bridge. Turn right across the river and WITH GREAT CARE cross the railway. Walk with the hedge on your right and the river on your left to a signpost where you turn right to reach a stile. Cross the road and go through a gate along a clear track uphill, with the trees on your right. Turn left along the Offa's Dyke Path when you reach a signpost just before a fence.*

1 *Knighton can be reached by train, on the scenic Heart of Wales line between Shrewsbury and Swansea. Motorists can find Knighton at the junction of the A488 with the A4113. This walk starts from the riverside car park which is signposted off West Street, down the side of the old school building, which now serves as both a youth hostel and the headquarters of the Offa's Dyke Association. Walk back from the*

5 *Turn right to walk with the hedge on your left. This soon becomes a clear track, passing a farm on your right and keeping the hedge on your left. Eventually you go through a gate to walk with the fence on your right. Cross a field to a gate ahead of you, walking parallel to the Offa's Dyke Path below on your right. Aim for the gap in the trees ahead of you.*

6 *Go through the gate in the gap between the trees and bear right towards a stile in the fence on your right. This is directly above the Offa's Dyke Path signpost you passed on the way out. Retrace your steps downhill, TAKING CARE across the railway again, but stay beside the River Teme all the way this time until you reach the riverside car park.*

Upper Lurkenhope Farm

Offa's Dyke

Ⓒ

Panpunton Hill

River Teme

Ⓓ

Ⓔ

Tref-y-Clawdd
(Knighton)

Ⓑ Ⓟ

Ⓐ

B4355

car park, away from the river with a cemetery on your left, to West Street and turn right to visit the Offa's Dyke Heritage Centre Exhibition at the far side of the youth hostel. Turn right as you leave this and walk across the recreation field towards an Offa's

Dyke Path signpost in the bottom left corner. Divert temporarily to visit a section of the Dyke, which is signposted on your left. Here, too, is the 'Commemoration Stone'. Return to the signpost and follow the Offa's Dyke Path down steps to the riverside.

Walk 5
YSTRAD FFLUR (STRATA FLORIDA)
3.8 miles (6 km) Easy

Monks and pilgrims once walked through the primeval oak forest to the abbey of Ystrad Fflur (Strata Florida), which was known as the 'Westminster of Wales'. You can follow in their footsteps, while also passing more recently abandoned lead mines. Part of this route is a courtesy path and it is important that you do *NOT* bring a dog - this is sheep country. Leave all gates as you find them.

A Ystrad Fflur (Strata Florida) means 'the way of flowers' and was named after the River Fflur which flows past the original abbey site about 2 miles (3.2 km) to the south-west. The Cistercian abbey of the Blessed Virgin Mary was founded in 1164 by Robert FitzStephen, a Norman, and was relocated in 1184 with a charter by Rhys ap Gruffydd, Prince of South Wales. Building wasn't completed until 1201. The bell was bought at a cost of 97 marks (64 66p) and two cows in 1254. Despite its Norman origin, the abbey became a great centre of Welsh culture. Its monks were renowned for their practical assistance to the poor, building bridges, stocking the Teifi Pools 3 miles (4.8 km) to the north-east with trout, and introducing sheep. King John (of England) gave the monks his royal licence to sell and export wool in 1212. The abbey is now in ruins, but its unique main west doorway has survived both the Dissolution of 1539, when the remaining eight monks were removed and the land acquired by the Stedman family, and earlier attacks, including its burning in 1294 by Edward I, who saw it as a stronghold of Welsh nationalism. It also suffered at the hands of Henry IV's army during the insurrection of Owain Glyndŵr in 1401. The English plundered it, stealing the holy vessels and tethering their horses to the high altar. They then smashed down the building and set it on fire, but the abbey was rebuilt. Its ruins are now in the care of CADW (entrance fee to the abbey and museum Easter-September, free admission to abbey only in winter).

Visit the graveyard to see an old yew tree associated with Dafydd ap Gwilym, Wales' greatest mediaeval poet. Dafydd is said to be buried beneath it, but this is unlikely as the tree is probably at least 900 years old. This fact didn't stop George Borrow (whose *Wild Wales* was published in 1862) saying a short poem to the tree when he passed this way in 1854.

'O tree of yew, which here I spy,
By Ystrad Fflur's blest monast'ry,
Beneath thee lies, by cold Death bound,
The tongue for sweetness once renown'd.'

The 14th-century Dafydd ap Gwilym was a better poet. When rebuked once by a friar for confessing his love for a maiden, Dafydd retorted:

'God is not cruel as old men say,
He will not damn us, though others may,
For the love we bear towards woman or maid ....,
Save only three, all the human race
Are born of a woman, in every place.'

The yew tree does mark a ley, or earth energy, line which goes from the high altar to the edge of the graveyard at the grave of the unknown tramp. This tramp died a pauper in the snow while walking towards Rhayader in 1929. He was buried like a prince at Strata Florida, however. Is it coincidence that his grave is on the ley, anciently an honour only for royal burials? His epitaph reads:

'He died upon the hillside drear
Alone where snow was deep
By strangers he was carried here
Where princes also sleep.'

Also buried here on June 18th, 1756, near the chapel, is the leg of Henry Hughes Cooper. His leg was severed in a stage coach crash, but he later emigrated to the U.S.A.!

B Abbey Consols or Florida lead mine, which flourished from 1855 to 1911.

C Pontrhydfendigaid means 'bridge of the blessed ford' and boasts two 'lion' inns (see walk **2**).

D Pen y Bannau, the 1157 ft (353 m) hill, is crowned by a hill-fort.

0   1 mile

0   1 km

4 Cross the stile, turn right and go ahead to a stile beside a gate which leads to an old track once used by monks and pilgrims. Stick to this track, passing a wood on your left and keeping a fence on your right. Bear left with this fence away from the wood to a gate in the fence ahead of you.

5 Go through this gate to a farm track. This is a private track but the farmer has kindly agreed to its use as a courtesy path, where you walk at your own risk, down to the bottom right corner of this field.

B4343

B4340

(D) ▲ Pen y Bannau 352

Pontrhydfendigaid

(C)

Dolebolion Farm

(B)

B4343
To Tregaron

Afon Teifi

(A)

P Ystrad Fflur (Strata Florida)

6 Continue down this track (now joined by the right of way) past ruins on your right. When the track turns right, however, continue straight on downhill on to a stile in the fence ahead. Cross a small footbridge and go ahead to a gate which leads to the footbridge over the River Teifi near the start. Retrace your steps to the car park.

1 Follow the ancient monument roadsigns to Strata Florida, 1 mile (1.6 km) east of Pontrhydfendigaid, where the B4343 meets the B4340 from Aberystwyth. Park opposite the abbey entrance and walk back past the telephone box to the gate on the left giving access to a footbridge over the River Teifi. Turn half-left after the bridge, go through a gate and walk with the river on your left. Avoid trampling hay as you follow a meadow path across four stiles and through a gate to a fifth stile which stands in splendid isolation, having lost its fence. Continue along the track.

3 Turn right, cross the road bridge over the River Teifi, pass the Red Lion on your left and walk past a turning to the Black Lion on your right. Opposite the Welsh Presbyterian church on your left, turn right down a narrow path at the side of R. Rees' grocer's shop. This path joins another to turn left and reach a track. Turn right off this track along a path through a small housing estate, with houses on your left and, mainly, bungalows on your right, to a gate ahead of you. Follow a track across a stream and walk with this stream on your left past a bungalow on your right to a gate. Pass a cottage on your right and walk to a stile in the fence ahead, about 20 yds (18 m) left of a gate.

2 Cross a cattle grid and turn left over a stile. Pass ruined cottages on your left, cross a footbridge over the River Teifi and bear right to a gate. Follow the road past a shop on your right to a crossroads.

17

Walk 6
CWM ELAN (ELAN VALLEY)
4 miles 96.4 km) Moderate

The Elan Valley, with its artificial reservoirs set in high moorland, has become known as the Lakeland of Wales. While the dams are impressive reminders of the engineering skills exercised in Wales at the turn of the century, the greatest gift the City of Birmingham (which built the dams) bestowed was the free access (by Act of Parliament in 1892) to unenclosed land in the Elan, for the purpose of enjoying 'air, exercise and recreation'.

This is now the most important inland area for birds in Wales. The residents that breed every year include Red Kite, Little Grebe, Goshawk, Sparrowhawk, Buzzard, Peregrine, Tawny Owl, Long-eared Owl, Green Woodpecker, Great Spotted Woodpecker and Lesser Spotted Woodpecker. Look out for them on this varied walk, which takes in the lake shore, the high moorland and the native oak forest.

A The Elan Valley Visitor Centre tells you the history of the area in the words of participating characters. The Afon Elan, a tributary of the River Wye, was renowned for its exceptionally clear water, while its tributary, the Claerwen, meant 'white clearness' in Welsh. It was no surprise when an expanding Birmingham looked to this area for a fresh supply of water, following Liverpool's example of creating Lake Vyrnwy in north Wales. Birmingham's scheme was much grander, however, with a chain of five lakes in the Elan and Claerwen valleys envisaged. Having bought the land and rehoused the few inhabitants, work began on building the dams in 1893. Edward VII officially opened the scheme in 1904 but the first four reservoirs didn't operate until 1907 and the fifth, Claerwen, was opened by Elizabeth II in 1952. Their weathered stone helps the artificial works to blend in with the landscape. The reservoirs and works form only a small part of the gathering grounds, which cover 45,000 acres (18,220 ha) or 71 square miles. With an average annual rainfall of 70 inches (1,780 mm), the 5 reservoirs impound 22,000 million gallons (101,200 million litres) of water. 76 million gallons (350 million litres) a day are pumped to Birmingham, flowing along 73 miles (117 km) of aqueduct by gravity at an average gradient of 1:2300, with inverted siphons to carry the water across large valleys such as the Severn. As Birmingham is 600 ft (180 m) above sea level, the beginning of the aqueduct had to be 770 ft (231 m) high. As the bottom of the Caban Coch dam is only 700 ft (210 m) high, the valve inlet had to be 70 ft (21 m) above the bed of the reservoir. A submerged dam, just before the entrance to the aqueduct, holds the water to a height of 82 ft (24 m).

B This wide track, with its zig-zag, was the bed of the Elan Valley Railway, which owed its short existence to the construction of the dams. It grew to 7 miles (11 km) after being opened in 1894 from the Mid Wales Railway just south of Rhayader. Interchange sidings were near the junction at Noyadd. Workmen's trains ran till 1906, but never strayed onto the Mid Wales line. Closure came in 1917.

C Caban Coch Dam is 122 ft (37 m) high and 610 ft (183 m) long. 29 million gallons (133 million litres) of water is released each day to maintain and regulate the flow in the Afon Elan. This water is also used to provide the village and water treatment works with electricity.

D Caban Coch Reservoir covers 500 acres (202 ha) when full.

E This viewpoint *would* have shown you Nantgwyllt, the house lived in for a short while by the poet Shelley, and his wife Harriet, before the valley was flooded. This house also inspired Francis Brett Young's novel, 'The House Under the Water'.

F Elan village was built to house the waterworks operators, key construction staff and the few local inhabitants who needed to be rehoused. The school was closed in 1978 and is now an Outdoor Pursuits Centre.

CWM ELAN (ELAN VALLEY)
Continued

0 _____ 1 mile
0 _____ 1 km

1 Park your car at the Visitor Centre, which is signposted with a red dragon symbol. This is on your left at the end of the B4518 as you come from Rhayader. There is an infrequent bus service from Rhayader. Turn right from the car park to cross the bailey bridge next to the unsafe suspension bridge. Go through the gate that would have been straight ahead if you could have crossed the suspension bridge and turn right along the track through the wood.

2 Follow the track as it zig-zags up, first turning sharply left, then sharply right. Walk past the dam on your right to the edge of Caban Coch Reservoir. Turn left to follow the distinct path over the slate along the side of the lake, which is on your right. When you reach a wooded inlet, turn left inland.

To Rhayader

Afon Elan

B4518

Elan Village

Ⓕ

Ⓟ

Ⓐ

Ⓑ

Craig-y-foel

Ⓒ Dam

Cnwch

Craig Cnwch

Caban Coch Reservoir

Ⓓ

Ⓔ

5 Turn left along this lane and walk beside broadleaved trees on your right as it bears right. Turn sharply left downhill when a signpost points to Elan Village, which you pass on the way back to the bailey bridge and the car park at the Visitor Centre.

3 Follow the path uphill, with the trees on your right. When the perimeter fence of the forest turns right, continue straight ahead. Walk past a clump of pine trees on your left, then turn left along the track to pass the trees and a ruined farmhouse on your left.

4 Continue along this track until it reaches a gate. This gives access to a quiet lane which you follow downhill, eventually going through a gate across the lane and turning left to meet another lane.

Walk 7
LLANDRINDOD
7 miles (11.2 km) Moderate

Nature and civilization combine to make this a memorable walk. The Lake at Llandrindod is only five minutes walk from the town centre, yet it is a beautiful haven for wildlife, especially toads and ducks. Llandrindod is situated 700 ft (210 m) above sea level, so it doesn't take long to reach the wind-swept uplands, with their magnificent views. Buzzards and kites may be seen. Humans have left their mark, with what look like ancient hut circles on the hills and evidence of an ancient stone circle in, appropriately, Temple Street.

Opposite is the Metropole Hotel, built to accommodate the many thousands of Victorians who took the waters here. The Romans were here too, with items from their fort of Castell Collen on display in Llandrindod Museum.

A Bailey Einon Woodland Trail was a winner of the 1983 Prince of Wales award for its outstanding contribution to the improvement of the Welsh environment. The trail gives access to a fine native (and now quite rare) deciduous wood on the banks of the River Ithon. The wood provides habitats for birds and small mammals, including tits, redstarts, pied flycatchers, voles, shrews and, sometimes, otters. Apart from the way they enhance the environment, the trees provide a continuous supply of wood through coppicing, providing useful local work.

B Cefnllys church is reached by what is still known as 'Shaky Bridge', despite the former very primitive kind of suspension bridge having been replaced by a sturdier structure (the old bridge never did let anyone down). The old church is well worth visiting, since it is in an ancient holy site, with a circular graveyard. Although isolated, Cefnllys used to be a borough. When the big new church of the Holy Trinity was built in Llandrindod in 1871, the scattered congregations of Cefnllys and Old Llandrindod were encouraged to worship in the new church by removing the roofs of the old ones. Local feeling led to them being re-roofed and restored in 1895.

C The hill that towers above the church is the site of Cefnllys Castle. This was probably an ancient hill-fort but Roger Mortimer, a Norman Marcher lord, built a strong castle here in 1242. The Welsh stormed it in 1262 only to be starved out by Mortimer, with 800 dead on both sides. Owain Glyndŵr burnt it down in 1406.

D This windswept hill bears traces of early settlement.

E Old Llandrindod church is where the first Archbishop of Wales was elected to office in 1920.

F The ground plan of an early church known as Llanfaelog, the church of St Maelog, was discovered in 1984, removed from Cefnllys Lane and recreated here by the Clwyd-Powys Archaeological Trust.

G Llandrindod Wells was the most fashionable spa in Wales in the Victorian era. While the chalybeate spring, known as the Rock Water, had been used for a long time, the saline and sulphur springs were re-discovered in 1732. Gaming houses, assembly rooms, the boating lake, string orchestras and a little race-course all helped attract 80,000 visitors a year, who came on the new railway. You can still drink the water in the summer, while the Victorian Festival every September recreates the heyday of Llandrindod Wells.

H Llandrindod Wells Museum is well worth a visit. It contains Roman remains from Castell Collen, the Roman auxiliary fort which overlooks the River Ithon, one mile (1.6 km) to the northwest. A dugout canoe, probably medieval, is also on view.

I The surrounding countryside is dotted with standing stones, stone circles and cairns. Llandrindod's ancient holy nature is emphasised by the traces of a stone circle in the gardens off Temple Street, opposite the modern conference centre of the Metropole Hotel.

J Holy Trinity Church is where Wales' Archbishops are now elected.

0 _____ 1 mile

0 _____ 1 km

1 *Llandrindod, which is on British Rail's scenic 'Heart of Wales' line. is at the junction of the A483 and the A4081. Park your car at The Lake, which is signposted at the end of Princes Avenue. Turn left and walk with the lake on your right to a signposted bridleway on your left. Go through the gate into the woodland. Fork right to follow the signposted footpath on your right. When you reach a fence walk with it on your left. Cross a stile ahead of you and turn half left across a field to a gate beside a public footpath signpost.*

2 *Go straight ahead through a gate, ignoring the track on your left. Turn half right across the field, follow the path beside the brook on your right and go through trees to a gap in the fence where a stile once stood. Bear slightly left, away from the trees across the field to a stile. Cross a young conifer plantation to a second stile. Turn left and walk to a stile at the end of the fence on your left. Cross an adjoining stile and walk ahead to a farm track. Turn left along this track. Follow the track around to the right to a waymarked stile in the fence on your left. Cross it to reach a road at another stile.*

3 *Turn right along this road. Keep right at a T junction and walk down to a waymarked stile on your left. Follow the direction of the yellow arrow to a stile in the bottom corner of the field. Turn left to walk the Bailey Einon Woodland Trail. Return to cross the Shaky Bridge over the river and follow the path to Cefnllys church. Return across Shaky Bridge to a picnic site on your left.*

6 *Walk round the lake, which is on your right, back to the car park. Turn left down Princes Avenue, then left down Temple Street to a signposted path on your right to the Rock Park and Chalybeate Spring. Return to Temple Street and turn left to visit the Museum, on your right after the Metropole Hotel. Cross the road to see the remains of a stone circle in the gardens opposite and to visit Holy Trinity church in Spa Road. Return to the car park.*

5 *Go through a small gate to pass Bank House on your right. Cross a stile on your right into the conifer forest. Turn left to walk with the fence on your left, then follow the track uphill through the forest to a lane. Ignore the stile opposite. Turn left along the lane to a signposted path on your right. Turn half left uphill, passing the summit cairn on your right, then down to a gate in a fence ahead of you and over a stile in the next fence. Turn left to cross another stile and drop down to the lane. Turn right along the lane past the old church on your left.*

4 *Turn right along the signposted forest walk from the picnic site. Instead of turning left into the conifers, however, go ahead through a gate along a clear path with a stream on your right. Continue with a hedge on your left to a gate leading to a farm track. Turn left uphill, keeping left at a fork, to a gate. When the track bends left just before a fence, turn right downhill with the fence on your left.*

21

Walk 8
CEMAES HEAD
5 miles (8 km) Easy

The Pembrokeshire Coast Path gives walkers the opportunity to enjoy 180 miles (289 km) of one of the most beautiful coastlines in Britain. Our walk goes around Cemaes Head, a bold promontory forming the southern arm of the Teifi estuary, at the northern end of the Coast Path. Fulmars, choughs and the occasional peregrine falcon may be seen, while grey seals frequently appear off shore.

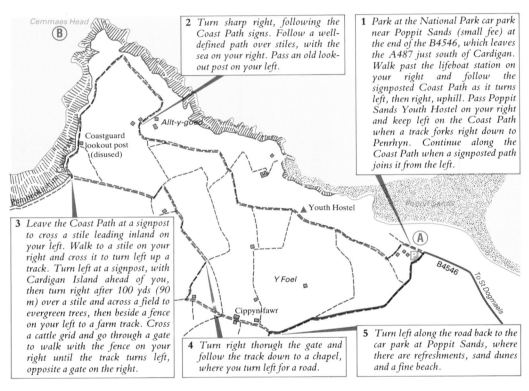

2 *Turn sharp right, following the Coast Path signs. Follow a well-defined path over stiles, with the sea on your right. Pass an old look-out post on your left.*

1 *Park at the National Park car park near Poppit Sands (small fee) at the end of the B4546, which leaves the A487 just south of Cardigan. Walk past the lifeboat station on your right and follow the signposted Coast Path as it turns left, then right, uphill. Pass Poppit Sands Youth Hostel on your right and keep left on the Coast Path when a track forks right down to Penrhyn. Continue along the Coast Path when a signposted path joins it from the left.*

3 *Leave the Coast Path at a signpost to cross a stile leading inland on your left. Walk to a stile on your right and cross it to turn left up a track. Turn left at a signpost, with Cardigan Island ahead of you, then turn right after 100 yds (90 m) over a stile and across a field to evergreen trees, then beside a fence on your left to a farm track. Cross a cattle grid and go through a gate to walk with the fence on your right until the track turns left, opposite a gate on the right.*

4 *Turn right thorugh the gate and follow the track down to a chapel, where you turn left for a road.*

5 *Turn left along the road back to the car park at Poppit Sands, where there are refreshments, sand dunes and a fine beach.*

A Poppit Sands lifeboat station has served this area for a century.

B Cemaes Head is noted for its seals. Two hundred or more years ago, however, this coast was renowned for its many mermaids. Here at Cemaes Head, a fisherman called Pergrin, in about 1800, found a mermaid in a cave combing her hair. He released her when she promised to give him three shouts when he needed them most. This she did, warning him to take up his nets to avoid a storm in which 18 others lost their lives. One mermaid was said to have been kept as an unwilling wife at Treseissyllt, west of Fishguard.

Walk 9
FELIN GERI
4 miles (6.4 km) Easy, but may be muddy in wet weather

0 _____ 1 mile
0 _____ 1 km

The Teifi is one of the most attractive rivers in South Wales. Here we visit the ruins of a castle overlooking a scenic bend in the river and walk through woods to reach a watermill which has survived since at least the 16th century. This is Felin Geri, which has its own restaurant.

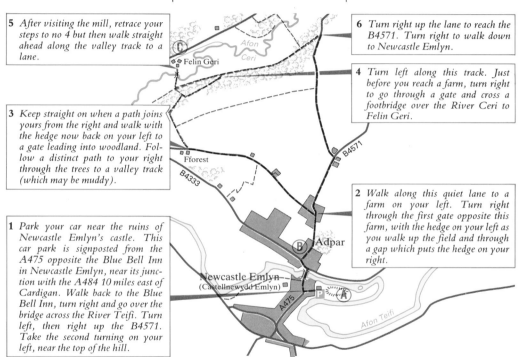

5 *After visiting the mill, retrace your steps to no 4 but then walk straight ahead along the valley track to a lane.*

6 *Turn right up the lane to reach the B4571. Turn right to walk down to Newcastle Emlyn.*

4 *Turn left along this track. Just before you reach a farm, turn right to go through a gate and cross a footbridge over the River Ceri to Felin Geri.*

3 *Keep straight on when a path joins yours from the right and walk with the hedge now back on your left to a gate leading into woodland. Follow a distinct path to your right through the trees to a valley track (which may be muddy).*

2 *Walk along this quiet lane to a farm on your left. Turn right through the first gate opposite this farm, with the hedge on your left as you walk up the field and through a gap which puts the hedge on your right.*

1 *Park your car near the ruins of Newcastle Emlyn's castle. This car park is signposted from the A475 opposite the Blue Bell Inn in Newcastle Emlyn, near its junction with the A484 10 miles east of Cardigan. Walk back to the Blue Bell Inn, turn right and go over the bridge across the River Teifi. Turn left, then right up the B4571. Take the second turning on your left, near the top of the hill.*

A Newcastle Emlyn, which has all the typical features of a small Welsh market town, is in old Carmarthenshire while Adpar, across the river, is in old Cardiganshire. Far from being 'new', the old settlement of Dinas Emlyn was named after a local chieftain. Llywelyn ap Iorwerth occupied the original castle north of the river in 1215. The 'Newcastle' was built by Maredudd ap Rhys in 1240, but was rebuilt by Sir Rhys ap Thomas after he was knighted by Henry VII on the battlefield of Bosworth on August 22nd, 1485. The castle was damaged by Parliamentary forces during a long siege in 1644 and was abandoned in 1648.

B Adpar elected its own M.P. until 1742. A plaque in the wall of a shop near the bridge records that Wales' first official printing press was located here.

C Felin Geri has been producing stoneground wholemeal flour since the 16th century. Unusually, it has two wheels in the same stream, with the second wheel being added in 1880 to drive a sawmill. There is also a play fort for children.

23

Walk 10
LLANDUDOCH (ST DOGMAEL'S)
7 miles (11.2 km) Easy, but may be muddy in wet weather

This walk starts from the car park at Poppit Sands, which is also the start of the Cemaes Head walk, so you could combine the two. Youth hostellers will find these two walks convenient to Poppit Sands Youth Hostel, while the beach here is a popular place in its own right, with a seasonal café. If you rely on public transport, and come outside July and August, start the walk at no 2 as buses only run further than St Dogmael's in the high season. The excellent views over the Teifi estuary are complemented by the abbey ruins and the old mill.

A Y Felin (The Mill) at St Dogmael's exists as an example of working history. Its position adjacent to the abbey suggests its original purpose. There is certainly a record of an early fulling-mill (pandy) in St Dogmael's in 1291, evidence of the early cloth trade in the lower Teifi Valley. This water-powered corn mill was first recorded in the 1640s. The road running between the millpond and the abbey was known as 'husk of wheat' ('Shin Grug' in Welsh) so it is reasonable to conclude that the monks worked a corn mill here. New machinery was installed in 1819 but the mill was derelict by 1952. It was restored in the early 1980s and the three storey mill now flourishes, producing wholemeal flour. There are guided tours.

B St Dogmael's is named after the 5th-century Celtic saint who came here. Our only link with that period is a 6th century memorial stone which is now kept in the parish church. It is important for providing the solution to the interpretation of the Ogham alphabet since it is inscribed, in both Latin and Ogham (old Irish), 'Sagranus the son of Cunotamus'. Other evidence was destroyed by the Vikings, who visited this coast regularly and put the village to flames in 987, leaving its ancient Celtic church in ruins. Perhaps this experience contributed to the inhabitants of St Dogmael's becoming noted as a fierce and hardy race.

In 1115, however, a dozen monks were brought here by one of the principal Norman conquerors of South Wales, Robert FitzMartin of Cemais. They were members of the Tiron Order, founded by St Bernard of Abbeville, who died in 1119. He lived an austere life, encouraging a rigorous regime of manual labour and a strict adherence to the Benedictine rule. This early monastery was elevated to the status of an abbey in 1120 and endowed with lands in Devon, Wexford (Ireland) and Pembrokeshire (notably Caldey Island). A glorious abbey was under construction when Giraldus Cambrensis and Archbishop Baldwin were entertained here by the Lord Rhys in 1188. The abbey was completed in the latter half of the 13th century and is recognised as being a superb example of the free-flowing English style. Such material greatness led to a decline in spirituality, however, with the monks becoming corrupted by high revenues and Gascon wine. There were only 3 monks in 1401-2, yet they were eating for many more! An abbot and 8 monks were in residence at the Dissolution. With its lands sold, the abbey buildings were plundered for stone. The north and west walls of the nave still stand to their full height, however.

C Cardigan Island, which comes into view just below the horizon, across the Teifi estuary, is a nature reserve owned by the West Wales Trust for Nature Conservation. It had an established puffin colony until a storm on 15th March, 1934 caused the wreck of the S.S. Herefordshire on the north-west corner of the island. The ship, which was built in Belfast in 1905, was being towed from Dartmouth to Glasgow for scrap. Rats from the wreck infested the island, killing the puffins. The island was treated with the exterminator Warfarin in 1968. The rats have disappeared and the birds are now returning.

D Look for the plaque to the Pembrokeshire Coast Path at Poppit Sands.

0   1 mile
0   1 km

1 *Park at the National Park car park near Poppit Sands (small fee) at the end of the B4546, which leaves the A487 just south of Cardigan. Walk back down the road, with the Teifi on your left, to Glanteifion. Turn left down a footpath after two two bungalows. Follow this path above the river on your left. Continue to the right of the football field and go down the road to St Dogmael's post office. Turn right down Church Street. Visit the mill on your left and the abbey and church on your right before passing the mill pond on your left.*

9 *Cross the road to a waymarked footpath opposite. Follow the hedge on your right and cross two stiles to a lane. Turn right down to Poppit Sands and the car park.*

8 *Turn right over a stile after 200 yards (180 m). Continue along the green lane above the stream on the left. Turn right after 250 yds (229 m) through a gate overlooking a caravan site. Follow the fence on your left to cross the stream by a concrete bridge. Go through a gate up to the caravan site entrance.*

7 *Turn left down the track just before Manian-fawr.*

6 *Go ahead at a crossroads, passing two houses on your right. Continue ahead along a rough track, with Cardigan Island coming into view.*

5 *Turn right after a mile (1.6 km) and right again, then left up a lane.*

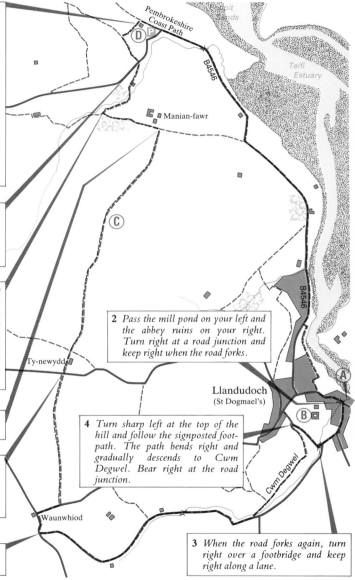

2 *Pass the mill pond on your left and the abbey ruins on your right. Turn right at a road junction and keep right when the road forks.*

4 *Turn sharp left at the top of the hill and follow the signposted footpath. The path bends right and gradually descends to Cwm Degwel. Bear right at the road junction.*

3 *When the road forks again, turn right over a footbridge and keep right along a lane.*

Walk 11
LLANFAIR-YM-MUALLT (BUILTH WELLS)
6 miles (9.6 km) Easy

'Llanfair ym Muallt' means St Mary's in Builth - a church dedicated to St Mary was built here during the 13th century. It was known as Builth Wells in English after Lady Hester Stanhope, the niece of the younger Pitt, stayed nearby and popularised the local spa waters, which were said to have been discovered by a party of mowers in 1830.

The waters are no longer drunk, but for one week every July, Builth is crowded with visitors to the Royal Welsh Agricultural Show, whose permanent site is on the northern side of the River Wye. Wildlife and fine scenery can always be seen, however, with the 'Wye Valley Walk' providing access to one of the most beautiful river valleys in Britain.

The River Irfon is also crossed. This tributary of the Wye is famous for its birdlife, which includes kingfishers, dippers, grey wagtails, coots, mallard ducks, moorhens and herons. Hares and rabbits may be seen in the fields, while grey squirrels abound in the woods. The river contains trout and salmon, and wild daffodils can be seen flowering in March.

A Penddol Rocks are typical of the magnificent rapids associated with the River Wye, and are at their best after heavy rain. View from the footpath only, however, as it is dangerous to try and clamber over them. *Heed the warning notices.*

B The grass-covered banks and mound are all that remains of Builth Castle. King Edward I had a strategically important castle built here to guard the important ford across the River Wye. Its predecessor, a motte and bailey castle built in 1098 by a Norman baron, Philip de Breos, had a bloody history, being captured and recaptured. Philip's earth castle reflected the hostile local conditions, which required a castle that could be built quickly using only local materials and labour. Philip built one of the largest castles of this type in Wales, as can be witnessed when you view the ditch. The castle is first mentioned as being destroyed in 1168 by the Welsh Lord, Rhys ap Gruffydd.
The Sheriff of Gloucester re-fortified it on behalf of King John,

who had repossessed the castle when the de Breos family fell into his debt. Two grandsons of Philip tried to regain their lands by plotting with the Welsh prince Llywelyn ap Iorwerth of Gwynedd. Giles, the Bishop of Hereford, retook Builth castle, while his brother Reginald cemented their alliance with Llywelyn by marrying the prince's daughter, Gladys. With the succession of Henry III to the English throne, the English barons no longer had a common cause with Llywelyn, who captured Builth from his son-in-law in 1218. When Llywelyn's grandson and Reginald's son, William, tried to enlarge his domain at the Welsh prince's expense in 1228, William fell prisoner to his grandfather and was released on payment of a 2,000 ransom and the promise that he would marry his daughter, Isabella, to David, Llywelyn's son by his second wife, Joan. The discovery of William's romantic relationship Joan in 1229 spoilt the happy atmosphere however, and Llywelyn had his grandson publicly killed. The marriage went ahead but without the agreed

dowry of Builth castle and cantref (a division of land), so Llywelyn seized it and held it until his death in 1240. John of Monmouth captured it in 1242 for the English crown, only for the Welsh to regain it in 1260 until Roger Mortimer captured it for King Edward I in 1276-77, when work began on the stone castle. A right-angled bank overlain by this castle may have been the remains of a Roman fort.

C The permanent site of the Royal Welsh Agricultural Show.

D Whilst in the area, do go just 3 miles (4.8 km) west along the A483 to Cilmery to see the monument to Llywelyn the Last, who was killed here by the English in 1282. His head was taken to the Tower of London, a symbol of the conquest of Wales.

LLANFAIR-YM-MUALLT (BUILTH WELLS)
Continued

0 _____ 1 mile
0 _____ 1 km

3 Go through a gate to a farm track. Pass the farm on your left as the track bears right, before turning sharply left. Follow this fenced farm track, with a forest on your right. Bend right with the track when it meets the railway and walk up to a minor road.

2 Cross a stile into a wood and proceed to grassland, with a fenced farm track on your left. Cross stiles and go through two gates until you draw level with the farm on your left. At this point a yellow waymark arrow points to a little footbridge over a brook, followed by a stile. Do not cross them! You leave the 'Wye Valley Walk' here to turn away from the river, left towards the farm, with the hedge on your right.

1 Builth is at the junction of the A470 and the A483. Park your car at the riverside car park beside the Tourist Information Centre near the Wye Bridge. The first half of this walk is along the waymarked 'Wye Valley Walk' going up river, so follow the riverside path with the river on your right. Pass playing-fields on your left and continue until a tributary of the Wye is met. This is the River Irfon. Turn left and follow it for 150 yds (135 m) to a suspension bridge on your right. Cross this bridge and ignore a stile on your immediate right but turn right at a waymarked gate beside a signpost at the corner of a road. Walk with a marshy patch, favoured by herons, on your right to the River Wye, where you turn left and walk with the river on your right. Continue along this waymarked path, crossing a stile and a small footbridge over a brook. Go through a kissing-gate and pass the rapids of Penddol Rocks on your right. Cross a stile and walk through trees to a bridge which carries the Heart of Wales railway across the River Wye. Walk under it.

Dolyrerw Farm

Wye Valley Walk

(A)

4 Turn left along this minor road and follow it back to where it bends right just before the suspension bridge over the River Irthon. Leave the road to go ahead across the suspension bridge.

Afon Gwy (River Wye)

Irfon

A470

(C)

A483

Llanfair-ym-Muallt
(Builth Wells)

Wye Bridge

(D)

P

(B) Builth Castle

5 Turn left to retrace your steps back to the riverside car park. Don't return to your car yet, however, as the walk continues to Builth castle. Cross the road and turn left towards the Wye Bridge.

6 Turn right opposite the Wyeside Arts Centre to cross another road to reach a signposted path to the castle, in between the Lion Hotel and Castle Corner wholefood shop. Walk around the castle mound and retrace your steps to the car park.

Walk 12
Y GELLI (HAY-ON-WYE)
4 miles (6.4 km) Easy

This is a ramble for all seasons from a unique little town situated only just inside Wales, and strategically placed in the Wye Valley. Hay is where the Wye Valley Walk rejoins the Offa's Dyke Path after their parting at Monmouth. There has been more than one route for the Offa's Dyke Path as it enters Hay from the south, however, and this walk takes in both of them. The *official* route is now the part at the start of our circular walk that hugs the English border. We return to Hay, however, along the old Offa's Dyke Path which is now known as the Castles Alternative Route. Needless to say, the waymarking is good, except for the brief linking path between the two, but this path is clear on the ground. The views on the return leg are particularly good, with Hay's old church standing out as a marker point. The walk includes patches of pleasant broadleaved woodland, while the final section into Hay is along an enchanting little stream. If you find you have some time to spare before or after the walk, you couldn't have chosen a better in which town to enjoy a browse through second-hand bookshops.

A The name 'Hay' is derived from the Norman-French word 'la haie', meaning a hedge. The sense here is of an enclosed settlement, for Hay was established as a Norman military town occupying a strategic position on the River Wye. The Romans had the same idea when they built a very large camp at Clyro just across the Wye to the north of Hay. The Norman, William Revell, seems to have started the present settlement in the early years of the 12th century. A church and a castle were built but the castle was soon relocated and built more solidly a few hundred yards to the east. It was accompanied by a walled town on its river-side. Despite being such a compact military stronghold, Hay suffered capture and burning on several occasions. King John was said to have destroyed the castle in 1215, but it rose from the ashes to be burnt by the Welsh Prince Llywelyn ap Iorwerth in 1231. Such destruction merely gave Henry III of England the opportunity to rebuild the castle in 1233 and to build new town walls in 1236. Owain Glyndŵr may have had a go as well before the Act of Union must have made Hay feel redundant. The castle and walls fell into disrepair, and a Jacobean mansion was built against it in the 17th century (this was gutted by fire in 1977). Hay would now be the typical sleepy country town if it didn't have one exceptional characteristic. In 1961 Hay became the Guardian of the Printed Word, or, rather, the Out-of-print Word. Richard Booth turned the town into a world-renowned centre for secondhand and antiquarian books – at the last count there were 18 book shops. There are miles of shelves and millions of titles. There is also an Independent Tourist Information Centre selling Hay's own flags and passports. Hay, of course, has its own king - Richard Booth. Hay isn't quite an Anglo-Welsh Andorra but it is different. A browse around its book shelves should produce a copy of the Kilvert Diaries, written by the Rev. Francis Kilvert, who was Curate of nearby Clyro from 1865 to 1872. Now established as a minor literary classic, they provide a valuable portrait of this area in the late Victorian period. Kilvert was a great rambler, and this walk follows in some of his footsteps.

B This is the current official route of the Offa's Dyke Path.

C This is the Castles Alternative Route. The exposed stone chamber that you pass is all that remains of a neolithic cairn once 60 ft (18 m) long.

D The bumps in the ground around here are the remains of a deserted Medieval village. Many such villages were abandoned because of the Black Death.

Y GELLI (HAY-ON-WYE)

Continued

6 Turn right along the road (B4350) into Hay-on-Wye. The second road on your right, just after the Hay Cinema Book Centre, is Oxford Road, where you started.

5 Continue along an old holloway but when this track veers left to a gate bear slightly right to a stile beside a cattle trough near the top of a dingle. Continue over stiles and through woodland to a field. Go ahead to pass through more woodland and the narrow part of a field into a larger wood. Follow the distinct path which gradually bears right so that you emerge from the wood opposite an old cottage. Pass the old cottage on your left, continue through a gate and bear left to a gate with the remains of a stile beside it. Go through it to turn half right and walk down towards Hay-on-Wye church. Keep left of the gorse bushes to find a track which takes you to the next field. Continue with an iron fence on your right and through a (lower) kissing-gate to walk beside a stream, which is crossed and recrossed several times.

1 Start from the car park off Oxford Road (the B4348) opposite the castle at Hay-on-Wye. The 39 bus between Brecon and Hereford also stops near here. Turn right from the car park towards the bus stop but turn right down the gated track opposite it. This is the Offa's Dyke Path and is waymarked with acorn symbols. Go through a kissing-gate to walk with the hedge on your left. Ignore a stile on your left and go ahead through more kissing-gates to walk with a hedge now on your right and then with a stream (Dulas Brook, the border between England and Wales) on your left. Cross a footbridge ahead and go over two stiles before veering right across the field to a stile. Turn left along a minor road.

2 Turn right off the road across a stile beside a gate and signpost. Walk with the stream on your right until a waymark post directs you to cross it by a footbridge. Continue with the stream on your left and go over a succession of stiles to reach a lane. Turn right here, leaving the waymarked Offa's Dyke Path. Walk past the farmhouse and go through a gate across the lane. Continue along the lane until it turns left.

3 Leave the lane at this corner to follow the path which goes straight ahead. Continue along the distinct path to a gate in a parting between the trees ahead. Pass Penhenallt farm on your right to reach a lane.

4 Turn right along this lane, which soon bends left to give a fine view of Hay-on-Wye on your right. When the lane turns sharply right, look for a stile beside a gate in the corner on your left. Walk ahead, as directed by the waymark arrow, to pass the exposed stone chamber of an ancient long barrow on your left.

Walk 13
DINAS ISLAND

0 _____ 1 mile
0 _____ 1 km

3 miles (4.8 km) Easy, but be careful on the cliffs

The 'island' of Dinas is part of the mainland. At the end of the Ice Age, however, a glacier in New- port Bay caused meltwater to flow westwards, creating a real island, with the beach at Pwllgwaelod being then a river estuary. The cliffs are exposed, showing evidence of folding.

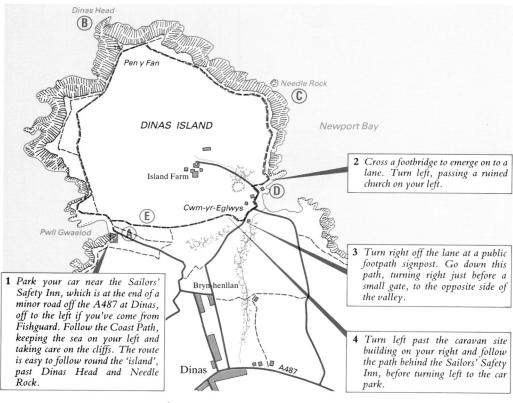

2 *Cross a footbridge to emerge on to a lane. Turn left, passing a ruined church on your left.*

1 *Park your car near the Sailors' Safety Inn, which is at the end of a minor road off the A487 at Dinas, off to the left if you've come from Fishguard. Follow the Coast Path, keeping the sea on your left and taking care on the cliffs. The route is easy to follow round the 'island', past Dinas Head and Needle Rock.*

3 *Turn right off the lane at a public footpath signpost. Go down this path, turning right just before a small gate, to the opposite side of the valley.*

4 *Turn left past the caravan site building on your right and follow the path behind the Sailors' Safety Inn, before turning left to the car park.*

A The Sailors' Safety Inn has shown a light after dark to help sailors in Fishguard Bay since 1593. An old lime kiln stands opposite it. Coasters used to bring limestone here to be made into quick-lime for local farms.

B Dinas Head is the highest point, giving views of Cemaes Head to the east and Strumble Head to the west. Dolphins and porpoises may sometimes be seen off-shore.

C Needle Rock is famous for its birdlife, with Great Black-backed Gulls nesting on the top, above Herring Gulls and Razorbills.

D The ruined church in Cwm-yr-Eglwys was a victim of the great storm of October 25th, 1859, which also saw the loss of 114 ships.

E This is the glacial meltwater channel, scoured from east to west.

Walk 14
PENTRE IFAN
4 miles (6.4 km) Easy

This is a walk through ancient broad-leaved woodland along old tracks and lanes to possibly the best known prehistoric monument in Wales. There are also magnificent views of the coastline and of Carningli, the mountain where St Brynach communed with the angels in the 6th century.

1 Park your car at the Salutation Inn, Felindre, on the A487 between Fishguard and Cardigan (and on bus route 412). Turn right along the grassy verge of the A487 for 400 yds (360 m), crossing the bridge, until you reach a lane on your left. Turn left up this lane, go ahead at a crossroads and continue to a T junction. Go ahead to a track.

2 Walk along the track, with Carningli on your right. Follow a signposted path to the right of a farm. Cross a stream and turn left off the track at a signpost. Follow yellow arrows over a stile on your right.

3 Go ahead with trees on your right to a waymark post. Follow yellow arrows right, then left. Keep to the waymarked track through the woods, swinging left, then right to a stile near a gate. Walk with the hedge on your left to a waymark post. Turn left, then immediately right to reach a waymarked stile beside a gate. Walk with the fence on your right to another stile and turn left to a road.

4 Turn left along this road until you reach a signpost pointing to your left, indicating a path leading to Pentre Ifan burial chamber. Turn left here.

6 Follow this track around to the left, then to the right. Cross the river by a concrete bridge to reach the road. Turn left along the verge for Felindre and the car park (or bus stop).

5 Return to the road and turn left. Walk along the road, bending right to a fork, where you bear left to a T junction. Turn right for 100 yds (90 m), then turn left up a signposted path. Ignore a turning to a farm on your left. Go ahead along a rough track.

A The cromlech or dolmen of Pentre Ifan is a great stone burial chamber. A large capstone is delicately balanced high above the ground on pointed supporting slabs. The capstone is 16 ft 6 ins (5 m) long and 9 ft (3 m) wide. It stands 8 ft (2.5 m) above ground and originally formed the roof of a Neolithic burial chamber which was covered by a mound 130 ft (40 m) long. About 5000 years old, it frames Mynydd Carningli within its upright boulders and capstone. Fairies are said to have been seen here, while a ley, or earth-energy, line goes through the chamber to Carningli.

B Carningli–1150 ft (351 m) high.

C Just one mile (1.6 km) east of Felindre is Castell Henllys, a reconstructed Iron Age village.

31

Walk 15
CNWCLAS (KNUCKLAS)
6.5 miles (10.4 km) Moderate

This walk affords fine views from a height of over 1200 ft (360 m) along clear ridge tracks between the valleys of the River Teme, to the north, and the River Lugg, to the south. But the finest views are from the hill above Knucklas, an ancient site connected with King Arthur, and once crowned by a Norman castle. Its remaining stones were incorporated in the impressive railway viaduct.

A Craig-y-Don wood is a mystical place. It is named after Don, the Celtic goddess who was married to the horned God Belinus. Their three children were Ceridwen, the Earth Goddess who married Llyr (King Lear), Gwydion the Enchanter (one of the three Golden Shoemakers of Britain) and Gilfaethwy. You can read about them in the fourth branch of *The Mabinogion*, the Welsh book of 14th century stories. The last man to be executed in old Radnorshire committed a murder near where the footpath leaves the road.

B An old race course was situated here, on the summit plateau. It was closed in 1861 but the farm where the track reaches the road is still called Racecourse Farm.

C This fine ridge track is part of 'Glyndŵr's Way', the 120 mile (192 km) long-distance path from Knighton to Welshpool, via Machynlleth. Named after Owain Glyndŵr, the great Welsh patriot and statesman who came close to establishing an independent Welsh state in the early 15th century, it is promoted by Powys County Council and is well waymarked with yellow arrows. It goes through the heartland of medieval Wales, linking places associated with Glyndŵr.

D This impressive viaduct carries the 'Heart of Wales' scenic railway line between Swansea and Shrewsbury. A feature of this line is its many small halts, enabling ramblers to walk from one station to another. The viaduct has mock castle towers at each end, perhaps in recognition of the fact that some of the stone used to build it was taken from the site of the ruined castle at Knucklas, which is on the top of the hill overlooking the viaduct.

E 'Cnwc las' is the Welsh for 'green mound', referring to the castle mound above the village. It is situated in a high, isolated spot and it comes as no surprise to find that it was the home of a race of giants. The local tribe was the Ordovices, who were known for their red hair and remarkable stature. When a tumulus a few hundred yards north of the castle mound, near Monaughty Poeth (Mynachty), was excavated in the 19th century, it was found to contain five skeletons, each of exceptional size. Perhaps these were among the last of an earlier, giant race whose existence until the 6th is recorded in Arthurian legend. The name Og or Gog refers to giants. A giant named Gogfran Gawr, who lived near Brecon, enlisted Arthur's aid when

his two sons were imprisoned here by the giants of Bron Wrgan (on the Shrophsire border). Arthur's reward for slaying these giants and releasing the two boys from captivity was the hand of their sister in marriage. Her name was Gwynhwyfar (Guinevere) and she was reputed to be a descendant of Ceridwen, the Earth Goddess. Arthur lived for a while with Gwynhwyfar in Knucklas castle. This may not have been the romantic attachment of Arthur's first marriage, however. It seems that Arthur had three wives, in succession, all called Gwynhwyfar. The sons (so important to a monarch of the Dark Ages) by his first wife were probably killed in Dyfed when Arthur was fighting the invaders identified as the Vandals in about 548. This date allows for the Celtic practice of dating their years from either Jesus' baptism by John or from His crucifixion, in the Gnostic manner. The Gwynhwyfar of Knucklas was probably his second wife, in about 550. Instead of new sons, however, she brought Arthur shame by carrying on an affair with Medrawd. The lovers fled to Perthshire, but Arthur caught them there and allowed his wardogs to tear them to pieces.

0   1 mile
0   1 km

1 Knucklas is a request stop on the Heart of Wales railway line between Shrewsbury and Swansea. It is on the B4355 road 2.5 miles (4 km) west of Knighton. Park in the village and walk back to the B4355. Walk along the road towards Knighton, crossing the railway.

2 About 300 yds (270 m) after the bridge over the railway, turn right through a small gate to follow a path uphill through Craig-y-don Wood. Ignore a tempting path on your left half-way up, but bear left near the top to a small gate. Continue along the path to emerge above the trees. Turn right, ignoring a ladder-stile in the fence on your left, and walk through a gate to a farm.

7 Go through a gate and turn right to walk beside the hedge up to the earthworks of the old castle. Retrace your steps to the village.

6 Turn right under the railway and fork left. Turn left over a bridge and turn left again just past the Bridge Stores. Walk with the railway on your left, then around a bend on your right. Go ahead along the track, ignoring a turning on your left to a farm. After 50 yds (45 m) ignore a path on your left to veer right along a hedged track.

5 Leave the waymarked 'Glyndŵr's Way' here by turning right along the lane. Turn left, downhill, when the lane forks. Follow this lane down to the railway viaduct on your right.

4 Follow the direction indicated by the yellow arrow on the gate, veering right beside the hedge to a waymarked gate. Continue along the track with the hedge now on your left. Turn right down a waymarked track to a gate which gives access to a lane.

3 Follow the farm track, veering left downhill to a road. Turn left along the road to a fork, where you bear right along a lane, ignoring a turning on your left after just 100 yds (90 m). Turn sharp right when the lane joins another at a 'Glyndŵr's Way' sign. Follow this track uphill for 1 mile (1.6 km) to a waymarked gate.

Ffrwdwen Brook

'Heart of Wales' Railway

Cnwclas Castle

E

D

P

B4355

Cnwclas
(Knucklas)

Craig-y-don
Wood

A

Craig-y-don

B

Bailey Hill

C

Little Cwm-gilla

Walk 16
SGWD GWLADUS
5 miles (8 km) Easy

This is an easy walk in the waterfall country of the Vale of Neath which you are positively encouraged to do on one of those wet days that Wales often provides. Rich in history, there is much evidence of this area's quite recent industrial heritage, and you will find yourself visiting the scene of a famous fairy-tale recorded by Giraldus Cambrensis in 1188.

A The Angel Inn, immediately behind which is the entrance to this waterfalls walk.

B This is the border land between the Old Red Sandstone mountains of the Brecon Beacons National Park and the coal measures which created industrial South Wales. It is the narrowest of transitional zones marked by outcropping bands of Carboniferous Limestone and Millstone Grit. As the Afon Nedd leaves the unyielding sandstone it slices through the limestones, forming a steep-sided gorge. On your left is a high sandstone outcrop, named the 'Farewell Rock' by miners in the 18th century, since it marked the end of the iron-ore and coal seams. The path was once the route of a mineral railway serving several small local mines.

C Shortly after your path crosses a small stream, notice a high waterfall through the trees on your left.

D Here are the ruins of a flour mill. Two fine millstone grit quern stones (hence the name of this rock, derived from northern England where it was extensively used to provide millstones) can be seen. The mill is also evidence that corn was grown here by local farmers until fairly recently.

E Notice a deep natural hole in the bank on your left, about 20 yards (18 m) after you cross a stile. This is lined with fungi in the autumn.

F Silica mining was an important industry in this area until about 1900. Silica was in demand from about 1820 when William Weston Young discovered how to make fire-bricks of exceptional quality and value from it. They were used for lining iron and steel-making furnaces, lime kilns and domestic fire places. You pass an old mine culvert with a brick tunnel in quite good condition (but too dangerous to enter). A chalybeate spring (the water contains iron) runs into the culvert. It is in this environment that an ancient folk tale seems to come alive. It was recorded by Giraldus Cambrensis when he passed this way on his 'Journey through Wales' in 1188. Elidyr, or Elindorus, was a 12 year-old being educated to be a priest, probably in the 11th century. Evidently a slow learner, Elidyr ran away from his lessons to escape his teacher's harsh discipline. He hid under the hollow bank of a river, generally accepted to be the Afon Nedd, without food for two days. Then two tiny men came to him, saying they could lead him to a land where all is playtime and pleasure. Not surprisingly, Elidyr followed them. They led him through a dark tunnel to an attractive land of rivers and meadows. Elidyr was presented to the king of these tiny people, who never ate flesh or fish but lived on the usual fairy dish of junket flavoured with saffron. They particularly hated lies and revered truth. Elidyr returned to our upper world at will and was allowed back to the fairy world unaccompanied. He told his mother all about it and she persuaded him to steal a gold ball when he next played with the fairy-king's son. He reached his home with it, but with the fairies in hot pursuit. Dropping the ball on his threshold, two fairies snatched it and rebuked him for breaking their faith in him. He tried to return to apologise to them, but could no longer find the underground passage. He eventually became a priest and Giraldus' uncle, David II, Bishop of St David's, often questioned him about the tale. Elidyr would always be moved to tears and repeat some fairy words.

G This beautiful waterfall is Sgwd Gwladus, named after one of the 24 daughters of King Brychan who, in the 5th century, gave his name to Brycheiniog. Gwladus had a son who became St Cadoc.

H The Upper Ddwli Falls are set in some beautiful deciduous woodland.

0   1 mile

0   1 km

4 *Go ahead across the footbridge over the Afon Pyrddin, with the Afon Nedd on your right. By so doing, you cross from West Glamorgan into Powys. Continue walking with the Afon Nedd on your right. As this direction is upstream, you can enjoy fine views of several waterfalls, culminating in the Upper Ddwli Falls. Eventually you emerge at the car park and picnic site by Pont Melin-fâch, which carries a minor road over the Afon Nedd.*

5 *You may well feel like retracing your steps for another look at the waterfalls. (There is an alternative route back to Pontneddfechan, however: turn right along the minor road across the bridge.)*

6 *Bear right at the road junction. Follow this road down to Pontneddfechan and the start of the walk.*

3 *When you reach the confluence of Afon Nedd and its tributary, Afon Pyrddin, notice the footbridge ahead but do not cross it yet. Turn left up the Afon Pyrddin, with the river on your right, until you reach a viewing platform. From this, observe the Sgwd Gwladus waterfall. Return to the footbridge.*

1 *Park your car in Pontneddfechan. This is at the end of the B4242 1 mile (1.6 km) north-east of Glyn-neath, which is 11 miles (17.6 km) north-east of Neath. There is ample roadside parking across the bridge after the Angel Inn. If you travel by public transport, there are a few buses (160 & 161) to Pontneddfechan from Neath, while Glyn-neath has a frequent service (X 5) from Swansea and Cardiff. Walk back towards the Angel Inn, where there is a very helpful seasonal Tourist Information Centre nearby.*

2 *Turn right to cross the old road with the Angel Inn on your left and the old road bridge on your right. Go through an iron gate to walk with the Afon Nedd on your right, passing information boards. Walk upstream along the clear path.*

Glyn-mercher-uchaf

Pont Melin-fâch

Glyn-mercher-isaf

waterfall

(H)

waterfalls

(G)

waterfall

waterfall

Gwernblaedda

POWYS

(F)

(E)

(D)

(C)

(B)

WEST
GLAMORGAN

Pontneddfechan

(A)

(P)

Walk 17
PEN Y FAN
7 miles (11.2 km) Strenuous (see page 4)

This is the hardest walk in the book and should not be attempted without proper preparation. It is not, however, so strenuous that it should disqualify many. A long, gradual climb is capped by a short scramble to the summit of Pen y Fan. This is the highest mountain in South Wales, indeed in Britain, south of Cadair Idris, at 2906 ft (886 m). The actual height climbed from the car park at Cwm Gwdi totals 1950 ft (595 m) and all that is required is stamina. *Do wait for a clear day, so that you may enjoy the views, and find your way safely.* Pen y Fan is a mountain, and those who climb to its summit will experience a real sense of achievement. Snowdon itself is only 654 ft (199 m) higher than this, the greatest of the Brecon Beacons.

A Cwm Gwdi used to be a danger area, with a Ministry of Defence rifle range. The nissen huts betray the army's continued presence, but rest assured that the danger warning on old maps *no longer applies.*

B 'Trig' points, or triangulation stations, are small white obelisks set up by the Ordnance Survey. They are used when measuring heights, surveying and mapping. They customarily command good views of the surrounding area, including in this case, a wide sweep from the Black Mountains to the Prescelly Hills and from Exmoor, across the Bristol Channel, to Plynlimon, near Aberystwyth. It may even be possible to see as far north as Cadair Idris on a very clear day. Pen y Fan is also famous for its distinctive sandstone summit. The steep northern face consists of a 'staircase' of rocks, with the harder ones standing out as steps. A very resistant blend of sandstones and conglomerates forms the plateau at the top.

C This obelisk marks the spot where the body of Tommy Jones, aged 5, was found. He lost his way between Cwmllwch farm and the Login on the night of August 4th, 1900. After an anxious search of 29 days his remains were discovered on September 2nd. The obelisk was erected by voluntary subscriptions that same year. It provides a very useful landmark in misty weather.

D Llyn Cwm Llwch is a textbook example of a glacial lake. An Ice Age glacier scooped out a basin at the bottom of the cliffs which became the lake. In ancient times it was believed to have an invisible island on which lived fairies. This could be reached through a door in a rock.

The Brecon Beacons.

0   1 mile
0   1 km

1 *Start from the car park at Cwm Gwdi. To reach this, go south-west out of Brecon, crossing the bridge over the River Usk. Pass Christ College and St David's Church, then turn left opposite the Drovers' Arms. This is Ffrwdgrech Road. Follow it under the bridge carrying the A40. Continue until you cross a bridge and the road divides into three. Fork left (signposted 'Cwmgwdi Camp') and after about 1.5 miles (2.4 km), ignore a roadbridge on your left and a turn off the road to your right by going straight ahead over a waymarked cattle grid. Pass army huts on your right to reach the small car park on the left. A footpath signpost directs you down to a stile which leads to a footbridge over the stream, Nant Gwdi. Climb steps and walk away from the stream, gradually ascending Allt Ddu, the left side of this valley. Bear right, following a distinct path which climbs up to the ridge. Other paths join it and a broad track unfolds along the spur of Cefn Cwm Llwch to the steep face of Pen y Fan, which is surmounted by a 'trig' point (a small white obelisk).*

3 *Retrace your steps to the start. This should make navigating easier in case of mist, but remain alert as paths fork away to disused quarries.*

2 *Carefully follow the ridge to Corn Du, where there is a low cairn. Continue with the steeper cliffs on your right. Look down on the glacial cirque that is Llyn Cwm Llwch. Go ahead to an obelisk erected in memory of little Tommy Jones.*

Cwm Gwdi Training Camp

(A)

Twyn Cil-rhew

Allt Ddu

Twyn y Dyfnant

Disused quarries

Disused quarries

Cefn Cwm Llwch

(D)

(C)

Craig Cwm Llwch

(B)

Pen y Fan 886

Corn Du

Walk 18
KYMIN NAVAL TEMPLE, SUCK STONE & BUCK STONE
6 miles (9.6 km) Moderate

The Forest of Dean covers the borderland between Wales and England east of the River Wye. Its broad-leaved trees enhance the valley, making this an area of outstanding natural beauty. It is also a secret forest, harbouring many ancient stones. Nelson's navy was built with trees from here, so the Naval Temple on top of the Kymin is appropriately located.

A The Naval Temple on top of the Kymin was erected as a memorial to the deeds of the Royal Navy from 1759 to 1801, when it was opened. Sixteen of Britain's greatest admirals are commemorated. The nearby Tower was built in 1794 as a banqueting room for the gentlemen of the Kymin Club. When Nelson visited this hill in 1802 he described the view as one of the finest he had seen. The town below is Monmouth, the birthplace of Geoffrey of Monmouth who must have had access to ancient and secret information to write his *History of the Kings of Britain*. The builders of the Naval Temple and the Kymin Tower must have had ancient knowledge too. Two ley lines cross at the Tower and at least four cross at the Naval Temple. The implication is that the builders chose these spots deliberately. They were built when William Blake, that great initiate, was writing his poetry and when Iolo Morgannwg, who wrote *Myverian Archaeology* and re-instituted the Gorsedd of Bards, flourished. The siting of these monuments shows a living tradition.

B The Suckstone is a large lozenge shaped stone block. It has fallen from the cliff above and is, reputedly, the largest single block of stone in Britain. It is about 3,500 tons in weight. Its name probably means a meeting place to discuss land matters (it is close to the border).

C Near Hearkening Rock is said to have acquired its name when local gamekeepers used it as an observation platform and listening post for poachers moving around in the woods below. There is a superb view from its top towards Monmouth, the Black Mountains and the surrounding woodland.

D The Buckstone, like the Suckstone, is a huge mass of conglomerate, or 'Pudding Stone'. This is older geologically than the carboniferous limestone of the Lower Wye Valley. The Ordnance Survey now have a trig point here, where there is fine view for surveying the surrounding land. On a clear day you can see for 60 miles (96 km) towards the Malvern and Shropshire Hills, the Sugar Loaf, the Black Mountains and the Cotswolds. Nearer, you can see the Newland meander, a large abandoned meander channel in the Wye Valley. The Buckstone itself is an ancient Druid 'Clacha Brath' or judgement stone. It could be easily moved in one direction, thus being called the rocking or buck stone. It was used for both divining and for sending messages. When pushed violently it would cause reverberations to travel through the strata on which it rested, giving warning of an enemy attack. It was both holy and lucky to touch the stone, especially to walk three times around it (clockwise). The Buckstone's quartz conglomerate nature means that it has interesting properties. Quartz can produce an electric current when put under pressure. When influenced by an electric field it will reverberate at frequencies measured in millions per second. The Buckstone no longer rocks as it was broken by hooligans in 1885, but its fragments have been cemented back together. Above it is the Sacrificial Stone. The basin in this may have held blood, but would also have collected dew and could have been a lamp or beacon.

0   1 mile

0   1 km

2 *Walk with conifers on your left to a forest track junction, where you turn left along the gravel track. When this makes a 'U' bend to your right, turn left along a rough path between two different types of* conifers. *Emerge through broad-leaved trees to a gravel track where you turn left to a crossroads. Turn right along a rough track, which bends left.*

4 *Walk up to this boulder, which is the Suck Stone. Climb up through the trees to its right and turn left to the Near Hearkening Rock. Climb around the corner to its top. Go ahead through the trees to a gravel track. Turn right down this, passing Reddings Lodge on your left.*

3 *When this track bends to the right, turn right up a path into the trees, just on the bend. Climb up through the trees, cutting across a similar path, until you reach a clear, gravel track. Turn right down this track for about 100 yds (90 m) until you see a large boulder above the track on your left.*

7 *Follow the clear Offa's Dyke Path across open ground, bearing left up to a stile. Cross it to a lane and turn left for 20 yds (18 m). Turn left over a stile into trees. Follow the fence on your right to an Offa's Dyke Path waymark. Turn left as indicated by the yellow arrow, climbing stone slab steps to a signpost. Turn right for Kymin Tower (and a fine view over Monmouth), the Naval Temple and your car park.*

5 *Continue along the gravel track. Pass a housing estate to reach the main road at Staunton. Turn right, passing the White Horse Inn on your left, then turn left up a lane. When you reach a wooden gate, turn right up the waymarked path, soon turning left to walk with a wall on your right. When you reach a triangulation point on your right, opposite a reservoir, turn right to the Sacrificial Stone, whose centre has been scooped out to form a basin. Just below this is the Buckstone. Descend through the trees to a broad track. Turn right along this down to the main road.*

1 *Park in the National Trust car park at Kymin Tower and Naval Temple. To get there from Monmouth cross the Wye Bridge and then fork left from the A466 along the A4136. Take the second turning on the left after this fork. Walk to the Tower and turn half-right to a stile beside a signpost which points to Staunton Road. Walk in that direction, through a belt of trees and down to a stile. Follow the clear forest track on your right to reach the A4136 road. Cross this road and turn left for 10 yds (9 m), then turn right along a forest path to reach a clear forest track, where you turn right.*

6 *Turn left along this road to a Gwent roadsign. Turn left up a lane just after this, following the signpost to Monmouth. When this lane bends left, go ahead along a rough track at the edge of the forest on your right. Follow this track as it turns right, then veers left to a clear forest track. Turn left along* this. *Pass the stile you crossed on your outward journey, on your left, as you go ahead along the track. When you reach a gate, veer right over a stile to walk with a fence on your left. When the conifers on your left give way to open country, turn left over an Offa's Dyke Path waymarked stile.*

Map labels: Suck Stone, Near Hearkening Rock, Redding's Inclosure, Redding's Lodge, Highmeadow Woods, Beaulieu Wood, Headless Hill, Staunton, Kymin Naval Temple, Buck Stone

Walk 19
PORTH YR OGOF
4 miles (6.4 km) Moderate

0 _____ 1 mile
0 _____ 1 km

This is a steep and adventurous walk along the tree-clad gorge of the Afon Mellte and Afon Hepste to see four spectacular waterfalls. Away from the rivers, there are panoramic views, while the start of the walk is marked by the Afon Mellte's disappearance into the huge cavern of Porth yr Ogof.

2 *Pass a pothole and cross a stile in a fence ahead. Hear the submerged river as you pass two 'collapsed entrances', then see the river at its resurgence on your right. Pass a meadow picnic-site beside the Afon Mellte on your right and keep the river on your right as you follow the path downstream. Ignore a footbridge on your right to follow a yellow arrow on your left. This waymarked path bears uphill, then descends to Sgwd Clun-gwyn waterfall.*

1 *Park your car at the car park at Porth yr Ogof, which is on a lane nearly a mile (1.5 km) south of Ystradfellte. This hamlet is 4 miles (6.4 km) north of Pontneddfechan (bus service) if you come up the Vale of Neath. Cross a stile on the left near the end of the car park (NOT the stile leading ahead). Walk down the well-trodden path to a warning notice and a seat. Turn left here to reach the cave, Porth yr Ogof. Return to the car park and cross the road to the signposted path opposite.*

5 *Turn left down the path waymarked in white to the water-falls. Turn left at the bottom to see Sgwd y Pannwr, then walk with Afon Mellte on your left upstream to see the miniature Niagara that is Sgwd Isaf Clun-gwyn. BE VERY CAREFUL as you follow the narrow path upstream to where your outer, uphill path with the yellow arrows is met again. Retrace your steps to the car park.*

3 *Follow the yellow arrow uphill to the perimeter fence of the conifer trees on your left. Follow this high path, with its panoramic views. Remember the point where a path which has white waymarks joins yours from the right, (where a sign points down to the Sgwd y Pannwr and Sgwd Isaf Clun-gwyn water-falls). Walk past it for now, however. Continue along the yellow waymarked path as it bends left. Turn right at a sign pointing down to Sgwd yr Eira waterfall, zigzagging down through the trees to reach it and follow the path behind the fall to give a spectacular view of the water.*

4 *Retrace your steps to the sign which points down to the Sgwd y Pannwr and Sgwd Isaf Clun-gwyn waterfalls.*

A Porth yr Ogof, 'the gateway to the cave', has a 57 ft (17 m) wide opening. Several people have been drowned here over the years, including experienced cavers. *KEEP OUT.*

B These potholes are also *DANGEROUS.*

C Take care when you view the resurgence of the Afon Mellte.

D Sgwd Clun-gwyn means White Meadow Fall. *BE CAREFUL* here as well.

E Sgwd Isaf Clun-gwyn means Lower White Meadow Fall.

F Sgwd y Pannwr means Fall of the Fuller.

G Sgwd yr Eira means Fall of Snow. It is famous for its path behind the water - *TAKE CARE* not to slip!

Walk 20
ABERHONDDU (BRECON)
3 miles (4.8 km) Easy

```
0                                    1 mile
├──┬──┬──┬──┬──┬──┬──┬──┬──┬──┤
0                          1 km
```

This is a pleasant, waymarked walk from the centre of the old county town of Brecon (now part of Powys). The Brecon Beacons Information Centre is passed, allowing you a chance to discover the many attractions of this national park. The mountains can be viewed in all their glory from the ancient earthwork called Slwch Tump.

1 *Start from the Wellington Monument in the centre of Brecon. This is near the bus stops and car parks, which are signposted off the High Street (turn down Tredegar Street, then right and left). Walk down Bulwark, away from St Mary's Church, to the Brecon Beacons National Park Information Centre on your left.*

2 *Fork left up Free Street. Continue past the Breconshire War Memorial Hospital on your right. When you reach a 'no entry' sign on your left, turn right up a red sandstone track.*

3 *Bend left with this clear track, ignoring waymarked stiles on your right. Continue uphill to pass a radio mast on your left. When you reach a gate ahead, leave the track to veer right uphill diagonally across the field, passing the earthworks of Slwch Tump on your right.*

4 *Cross a waymarked stile ahead of you in the top right corner of this field. Walk with the hedge on your right for 30 yds (27 m), then turn right over a stile and walk round the foot of the Tump on your right, with mountain views on your left.*

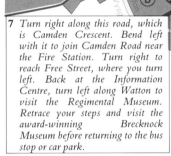

Aberhonddu
(Brecon)

Slwch Tump

B4601

7 *Turn right along this road, which is Camden Crescent. Bend left with it to join Camden Road near the Fire Station. Turn right to reach Free Street, where you turn left. Back at the Information Centre, turn left along Watton to visit the Regimental Museum. Retrace your steps and visit the award-winning Brecknock Museum before returning to the bus stop or car park.*

6 *Bear right to enter the next field to walk with the hedge on your left to a waymarked stile beside a gate. Cross this and immediately turn left over another stile. Walk with the hedge on your left downhill to cross a stile and reach a road.*

5 *When you reach a fence ahead, turn left downhill with a bluebell wood behind the fence on your right. Turn right over the waymarked stile at the bottom of this wood and walk with a fence on your left (ignore the stile in it) and the wood on your right. Cross a waymarked stile out of the wood to follow a fence on your left.*

A The Brecon Beacons National Park was designated in 1957 and covers 519 square miles (1344 square km). Its greatest peak, Pen-y-Fan (see Walk 17) towers above Brecon like a petrified wave of Old Red Sandstone. The town (and the old county) took its name from Brychan, the 5th century prince who came from Ireland and was a relative of King Arthur.

B The ancient earthwork called Slwch Tump is where Elyned, the youngest of Brychan's 24 daughters, suffered martyrdom. A chapel dedicated to her used to stand on the north side of the hill, which was also called Penginger. This would be a corruption of Pen Cefn-y-gaer (the head of the ridge of the fort).

C The Regimental Museum of the South Wales Borders is open daily from Monday to Friday (and on Saturdays from April to September).

D Brecknock Museum is well worth a visit. The dug-out oak canoe from Llangorse Lake is relevant to walk 22, as is the model of the settlement on the lake. There are also old inscribed stones, dating from the time of the Roman occupation (they had a fort at Gaer, west of Brecon) to the 10th century. A 6th century stone to Turpillins is inscribed in both Ogham and Latin.

E Brecon can also boast a cathedral (a 13th century priory church) and remnants of a Norman castle.

NANHYFER (NEVERN)

3.5 miles (5.6 km) Easy

Nevern is a small village with an ancient church dedicated to the Irish saint, Brynarch, who was a contemporary of St David in the 6th century. A fine Celtic cross 13 ft (4 m) high and which dates from around the year 1000 stands in the churchyard. Known as St Brynach's Cross, it is famous for the story of the cuckoo which arrived to perch on it on April 7th every year. This is the patron saint's feast day and the service wouldn't start until the cuckoo had arrived. One year it was very late and was found dead from exhaustion after the service, so hard had it flown against the storms to reach the church on time. This is a magical walk, along an old coach road, leafy lanes and passing many places of interest. The views over the surrounding countryside are superb.

A This hotel is Llwyngwair Manor and dates from the 15th century. It was the family home of the Bowens. The family line died out recently and the old farm is now a caravan park.

B Castell Nanhyfer (Nevern Castle) was built in the early 12th century by Robert FitzMartin, the Marcher Lord of Cemaes. It was captured and recaptured in fighting between Robert's grandson William, a Norman, and the Welsh Lord Rhys, despite William being married to Angharad, Rhys' daughter. The castle may have been built on an old Iron Age earthwork. A high motte was built in the west corner, with a small stone tower at the summit. The adjacent bailey or enclosure was well-protected by natural slopes, while there may have been a keep or rectangular tower in the east corner of the bailey.

C Follow the sign on your right at the hairpin bend as you walk down to Nevern. This directs you to the Pilgrims' Cross, which is about 30 yds (27 m) along the path, cut in relief on a rock face on your right. There is a kneeling place below it, to remind you to say a prayer. This was a wayside shrine on the pilgrims' route from Holywell to St David's.

D Nevern's church and churchyard contain so much of interest that Professor Sir John Rhys wrote: "Such a group of antiquities at one small centre is very remarkable." The Celtic cross is one of the best exaples of its kind in Wales, although it seems to have a Viking influence. On all sides are intricate geometrical carvings. This is the cross upon which the cuckoo perched on each St Brynach's Day, April 7th. It was probably erected to commemorate a 10th century local chieftain. Also in Nevern churchyard, near the porch, stands the Vitalianus Stone. It is inscribed in both Ogham (old Irish) and Latin as the stone of Vitalianus. Vitalianus was also known as Vortimer and he was the son of Vortigern, the drunkard high-king of the Britons who invited the Saxons Hengist and Horsa to help him against the Picts and Scots in about 450 AD. This gave the Saxons a foothold for their subsequent conquest of eastern Britain. Nevern was a very sacred place, fit for royal burials.

The mystical atmosphere of Nevern church is enhanced by the yew trees that surround it. An avenue of these leads from the churchyard gate to the porch of the church. The second tree on the right mysteriously bleeds - look for the blood red resin. Also in the churchyard is an epitaph on a wall tombstone in the second enclosed graveyard:

Anna Letitia and George, infant children of the Rev. D. Griffiths, Vicar 1783-1834.
'They tasted of life's bitter cup,
Refused to drink the potion up,
But turned their little heads aside,
Disgusted with the taste, and died.'

Nearby is the memorial to the Rev. John Jones, who was the bard 'Tegid'. He helped Lady Charlotte Guest translate *'The Mabinogion'* into English. Many of the unique tales in this great Welsh contribution to literature are set in this county of Dyfed. Perhaps the item which arouses most curiosity is the memorial stone to Maglocunus. This is embedded in a windowsill inside the nave of the church, on the right as you walk towards the altar. It is inscribed in both Ogham and Latin, saying:
'The monument of Maglocunus son of Clutorius'.

0   1 mile

0   1 km

4 *Go right along the lane and turn right when you reach a T junction. Bear left with this lane, ignoring a farm track straight ahead at a corner. When you reach a quiet, minor road, turn right and right again after 50 yds (45 m) at another road junction.*

5 *Pass a farm on your right before the site of Nevern Castle on your left. Continue downhill to a sharp bend on your right, where a sign directs you to the Pilgrims' Cross. Continue down to Nevern church and the Trewern Arms.*

1 *Park your car at the Trewern Arms, just before Pont y Nevern (Nevern Bridge) on the B4582 0.5 miles (0.8 km) north of its junction with the A487 at Temple Bar, mid-way between Cardigan and Fishguard. Turn left to walk up the road to a public footpath signpost and stile on your left just before Nevern bridge. Turn left and cross the field, veering away from the river to a clear track through the trees ahead of you. Follow this track between two fields and through gates into more woodland. Bear right with the track to reach a lane at a public footpath signpost.*

Cwm Cenau

Pont Newydd

Castell Nanhyfer Ⓑ

Ⓒ Ⓓ

Nanhyfer
(Nevern)

Pont y Nevern

Ⓟ

Ⓐ

Afon Nyfer

3 *Cross Pont Newydd (New Bridge) and pass a cottage on your left. Ignore the signposted footpath on your right (which is liable to flooding) but continue straight ahead along the track until you reach the corner of a lane.*

2 *Turn right up this lane, passing a hotel and caravan park on your left. When the lane bends right, go straight ahead on the track signposted 'Pont Newydd'.*

Temple Bar

A487 To Cardigan

Such bilingual inscriptions helped to provide a key to the Ogham alphabet. The Ogham form of writing was made by cutting notches along the edges of stones and probably originates from southern Ireland.

Maglocunus was the Latin form of Maelgwn. Maelgwn Gwynedd was the king of North Wales and the overall warlord of the British

after the death of Arthur in the 6th century. Maelgwn was the original Sir Lancelot and this *may* be his tombstone. Nevern church was associated with King Meurig ap Tewdrig, the father of the great Arthur and it is a royal burial ground, while Maelgwn Gwynedd granted land to Nevern church. His father is generally considered to be Cadwallon Lawhir, not

Clutorius, however.

In another windowsill is the Cross Stone, bearing an unusual relief cross. A consecration cross can also be seen outside on the north side of the church. By the church gate is one of only two old mounting blocks left in Pembrokeshire.

Walk 22
LLYN SYFADDAN
3.5 miles (5.6 km) Easy

Llyn Syfaddan, or Llangorse Lake, is the largest natural lake in South Wales. The bed of the lake is a basin scooped out of the rock by ice during the ice ages. The Afon Llynfi flows into it from the south and out again on the north on its way to join the River Wye. The old story is that because of evil deeds done by the ancient lake dwellers, the virtuous little river will not mingle its waters with those of the lake and so flows through the lake and out again. The footpath around the western side of the lake from Llangorse to Llangasty Talyllyn does not follow the shore very closely, as the height of the lake varies with the extent of the flood water. It is a lake of reeds and swampy borders – an ideal place for fen and water birds and vegetation, including white and yellow water lily.

2 *Cross the footbridge, turn half left and walk to a stile which is waymarked with a yellow arrow. Continue as directed to reach a ladder stile over a wall. Cross the next field to a stile preceded by a footbridge in the far corner.*

3 *Cross the stile and turn half left to reach a waymarked stile in the next hedge. Bear slightly left to a stile beside a gate in the corner of the field before a wood, with the lake on your left.*

4 *Cross the track to go along a forest path to a waymark post. Follow the path around the edge of the wood on your left. Cross a footbridge to go back into the wood and reach a waymarked stile.*

5 *Continue along the edge of the field, with the wood on your left. Cross another stile to go ahead, with the lake on your left, to a stile in the hedge which gives access to a lane. Turn right for Llangasty-Talyllyn church.*

6 *After visiting the church, go down to the lakeshore. In the absence of a right of way around the rest of the lake, retrace your steps but turn right at the car park to go down to the lakeshore where you can hire a boat, or see the prehistoric crannog or artificial island.*

1 *Park at the signposted car park near Llangorse Lake. This is reached by turning off the A40 road about 2 miles (3.2 km) east of Brecon, following the roadsign to Llangorse. Just before you enter the village, turn right to the signposted Llangorse Lake. Walk across the field on your right to a footbridge.*

To Langors

Afon Llynfi

P

Llangorse Sailing Club

C

Bwlc Crannog

D

Llyn Syfaddan
(Llangorse Lake)

A

Llangasty
Talyllyn

B

Afon Llynfi

A Giraldus Cambrensis wrote of the legend of the birds of Llangorse, that they would sing only for the rightful ruler of Wales. The birds ignored the Norman conquerors, Milo and Payn FitzJohn, but sung for the dispossessed Gruffydd ap Rhys who was of Welsh princely descent.

B Langasty-Talyllyn means 'the parish of St Gastyn at the edge of the lake'.

C Llangorse Lake is ideal for water sports. Boats are available for hire (telephone 087484-226).

D Ancient lake dwellers built this crannog or artificial island.

Walk 23
LLANTHONY PRIORY
2 miles (3.2 km) Easy

```
0                                          1 mile
|----|----|----|----|----|----|----|----|
0                          1 km
```

Llanthony is derived from Llan-Honddu (the church on the Honddu) or, more fully, Llan-Dewi-Nant-Honddu (the church of St David on the River Honddu). It is situated in the beautiful Vale of Ewyas, sandwiched between the ridges of the Black Mountains, with the Offa's Dyke Path on the eastern ridge and the Cambrian Way on the western.

4 Walk downhill with conifer trees on your left, then bend right to cross three stiles (beside gates) in succession and past a ruined building (Landor's House) on your right.

3 Veer left uphill to the top of the trees. Cross two stiles in successive fences on your left and walk uphill to a waymark post. Ignore the arrow directing you to the Offa's Dyke Path on the ridge of the Black Mountains above. Turn right along the path to a gate.

2 Cross this stile and turn right to walk with the wall on your right to another stile beside a gate. Cross this and follow the well-worn track ahead, away from the priory. Cross a stream and leave this track to bear left as directed by a yellow arrow to another stile beside a gate. Go over the bridge into the next field. Turn half-right uphill to a stile beside a gate ahead.

5 Continue along the well-trodden path, keeping the fence and trees on your right. Cross a stile to pass farm buildings (Wiral) on your right, bearing left to a stile. Continue with the fence on your right until you reach a stile in it (tucked behind a wall).

6 Turn right across this stile and walk with the fence on your left downhill to a stile which leads into woods. Bear right along the clear woodland path down to a stile beside a gate. Continue downhill towards the priory. Cross a stile and walk with the wall of the priory on your left back to the start.

1 Start from the car park at Llanthony Priory. This will be found by turning left off the A465 at Llanvihangel Crucorney, about 5 miles (8 km) north of Abergavenny. Llanthony Priory is signposted about 6 miles (9.6 km) on the right. Walk back from the car park past the priory and the Abbey Hotel on your right and Llanthony church on your left to a waymarked stile beside a gate ahead of you.

Map labels: Siarpal, (B), Wiral, (C), Priory Llandewi Nanthodni, (A), Llanthony

A Llanthony Priory was founded by Hugh de Lacy, Earl of Hereford, in 1108, after his kinsman William had already lived there as a hermit for some years. A community of Augustinian canons arose. These canons were all priests but were organised on monastic lines. They went out and preached in churches in which they were responsible for maintaining services. Despite their desire for poverty, the canons acquired wealth and endowments.

Then a period of unrest and warfare led to the rise of a daughter house at Gloucester, under the patronage of Milo, Earl of Hereford. The canons came to prefer the bustling life of the city and visits to the remote mother house were unpopular. Books and other possessions were removed to Gloucester. A revival in the fortunes of the de Lacy family led to rebuilding between about 1175 and 1230. Giraldus Cambrensis visited Llanthony in 1188 and passionately championed its simple life in contrast to that of its more wordly daughter house. The priory's lands were wasted during Owain Glyndŵr's rebellion and the house was dissolved in 1538.

B Walter Savage Landor, a writer and contemporary of Wordsworth and Shelley, built the house whose ruins are passed on your right.

C The walk through this wood may give you the chance to see a wood warbler, which has a yellow breast and a white belly.

Walk 24
Y-FAL (SUGAR LOAF)
3.5 miles (5.6 km) Moderate

There are three deservedly popular peaks around Abergavenny. The Sugar Loaf is the highest, just beating Blorens and Ysgyryd

Fawr. At 1955 ft (596 m) it just fails to reach the magic height of 2000 ft (609 m), but its long approach and summit views make

it appear higher. Its cone shape led to the belief, until the early 19th century, that it was an extinct volcano.

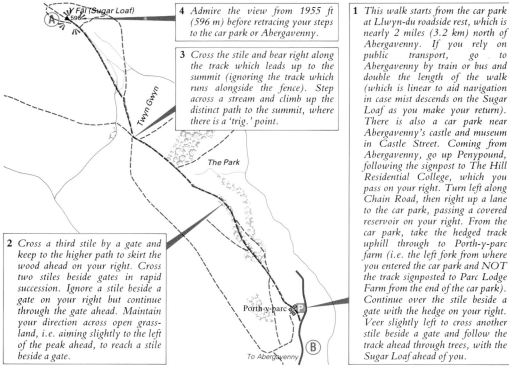

4 Admire the view from 1955 ft (596 m) before retracing your steps to the car park or Abergavenny.

3 Cross the stile and bear right along the track which leads up to the summit (ignoring the track which runs alongside the fence). Step across a stream and climb up the distinct path to the summit, where there is a 'trig.' point.

The Park

Twyn Gwyn

2 Cross a third stile by a gate and keep to the higher path to skirt the wood ahead on your right. Cross two stiles beside gates in rapid succession. Ignore a stile beside a gate on your right but continue through the gate ahead. Maintain your direction across open grassland, i.e. aiming slightly to the left of the peak ahead, to reach a stile beside a gate.

Porth-y-parc

To Abergavenny

1 This walk starts from the car park at Llwyn-du roadside rest, which is nearly 2 miles (3.2 km) north of Abergavenny. If you rely on public transport, go to Abergavenny by train or bus and double the length of the walk (which is linear to aid navigation in case mist descends on the Sugar Loaf as you make your return). There is also a car park near Abergavenny's castle and museum in Castle Street. Coming from Abergavenny, go up Penypound, following the signpost to The Hill Residential College, which you pass on your right. Turn left along Chain Road, then right up a lane to the car park, passing a covered reservoir on your right. From the car park, take the hedged track uphill through to Porth-y-parc farm (i.e. the left fork from where you entered the car park and NOT the track signposted to Parc Lodge Farm from the end of the car park). Continue over the stile beside a gate with the hedge on your right. Veer slightly left to cross another stile beside a gate and follow the track ahead through trees, with the Sugar Loaf ahead of you.

A The view from the top of the Sugar Loaf is superb, so reserve this walk for a clear day in order to appreciate it fully. The large mass of the Black Mountains can be seen to the north, while to the west lies the Usk Valley, Crickhowell and the Brecon Beacons. To the east can be seen Ysgyryd Fawr and eastern Gwent, with the Malverns

and Cotswolds in the far distance.

B Unsurprisingly for a Welsh border town, Abergavenny's chief feature is its castle. This is well worth a visit, if only to see the museum which is housed within its ruins. Your ticket to Abergavenny Museum can also be used, within a fortnight, to visit

the museums at Chepstow (Walk 39) and Monmouth (near Walk 19). A Norman castle was built at this strategic site at the confluence of the rivers Gavenny and Usk in about 1090. In 1175, Welsh chieftains were massacred here as defenceless guests at a Christmas banquet.

Walk 25
THE CLYDACH GORGE
2.5 miles (4 km) Easy

0   1 mile

0   1 km

South Wales was the industrial heartland of the British Empire, where ironmaking started, harnessing water power and using timber for fuel. Yet remnants of the original beechwood still survive, and much of this walk accompanies a delightful river with waterfalls.

1 *Start from the Clydach Gorge car park and picnic area (unless you come by bus - see **2**). To reach this, take the A456 Heads of the Valleys road between Abergavenny and Brynmawr. About 4 miles (6.4 km) west of Abergavenny and 3 miles (4.8 km) east of Brynmawr, turn south up a minor road signposted 'Caravan site'. This is Station Road, Clydach. The car park is on your right, just beyond the caravan site. Walk back down the road, passing the caravan site on your left.*

2 *Turn left at a footpath signpost to cross Afon Clydach by a bridge. Go ahead to cross the Heads of the Valleys road taking GREAT CARE. The bus stop here is for the X4 service (Cardiff-Abergavenny) and is where bus passengers start and finish this walk. Continue along the footpath*

3 *Follow the narrow path ahead, with a fence on your left and a hedge on your right. Continue through a wood with the river on your right. Pass a footbridge on your right, but keep straight on along the path. Go through a waymarked gate beside a signpost (notice the waterfall on your right). Continue over a stile and reach a road coming in on your left. This was the Clydach Railroad,*

towards a gate beside a signpost. Turn right on what was the Llammarch Tramroad (built to link the Clydach Ironworks with the canal at Gilwern). Do not follow the road uphill on your left, but keep

7 *Continue along this quiet minor road, which is now on the main route of the Clydach Railroad, which comes in on your left from the tunnel under the canal. Go on past the cottages of Maesygwartha.*

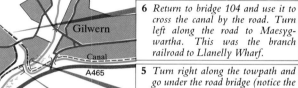

6 *Return to bridge 104 and use it to cross the canal by the road. Turn left along the road to Maesygwartha. This was the branch railroad to Llanelly Wharf.*

5 *Turn right along the towpath and go under the road bridge (notice the number - 104). Walk about 150 yds (135 m) further along the towpath to see old limekilns on the opposite bank.*

4 *Go ahead through the tunnel and turn sharp right to climb up the bank by the steps. These lead to the towpath of the Monmouthshire and Brecon Canal.*

which came down the valley from Gelli-Felen collieries and ironworks at Beaufort to Glangrwyney Forge in the Usk valley. Built in 1794, this predated the canal - hence the tunnel ahead.

Turn left down a steep, narrow, winding lane, past Clydach House on your left. At the bottom of the hill the road bends to the right for you to retrace your steps to the start of the walk.

straight on until this road bears right. Bear left here, where the gate is signed 'Forge House', at a footpath signpost.

A This was the site of Llanelly Furnace, established in the 17th century by the Hanbury family of Pontypool.

B Clydach House was the fine 17th century home of the Clerk to the Furnace. One, Francis Lewis, had his arms displayed over the main entrance (dated 1693).

C Llanelly Forge stood here to receive the pig-iron from the furnace. Large quantities of water were required to produce wrought iron.

BLORENS (BLORENGE)
4 miles (6.4 km) Easy

This is Cordell country, the setting for 'Rape of the Fair Country', a novel which is required reading if you wish to gain an understanding of the Chartist Rebellion and the industrial revolution in South Wales. It's easy to imagine Iestyn or Morfydd Mortymer (characters in the book) beside you as you walk this peaceful moorland with its inspiring views. *For safety, reserve this walk for a fine day.*

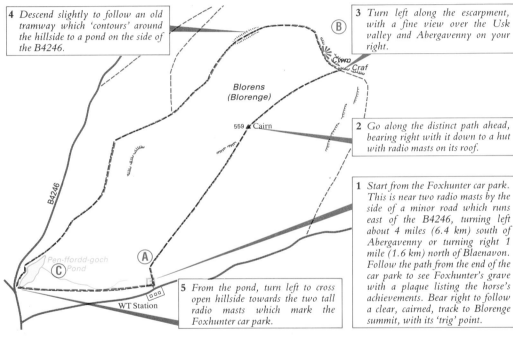

4 *Descend slightly to follow an old tramway which 'contours' around the hillside to a pond on the side of the B4246.*

3 *Turn left along the escarpment, with a fine view over the Usk valley and Abergavenny on your right.*

2 *Go along the distinct path ahead, bearing right with it down to a hut with radio masts on its roof.*

1 *Start from the Foxhunter car park. This is near two radio masts by the side of a minor road which runs east of the B4246, turning left about 4 miles (6.4 km) south of Abergavenny or turning right 1 mile (1.6 km) north of Blaenavon. Follow the path from the end of the car park to see Foxhunter's grave with a plaque listing the horse's achievements. Bear right to follow a clear, cairned, track to Blorenge summit, with its 'trig' point.*

5 *From the pond, turn left to cross open hillside towards the two tall radio masts which mark the Foxhunter car park.*

A Foxhunter's grave is marked by a plaque on a rock inscribed in memory of this champion international show jumping horse. Born in 1940, Foxhunter won 78 international competitions, including many foreign Grand Prix and the King George V Gold Cup (in 1948, 1950 and 1953). Having won bronze medals at the London Olympics in 1948, Foxhunter was a member of the team that won the gold medal at Helsinki in 1952.

B This magnificent view includes the old Monmouthshire and Brecon Canal at the foot of the Blorenge. The canal bank is haunted here. A woman in black was seen to vanish before the eyes of a man, his wife and two children in 1899. One of the children was then aged 12 and could still relate the event forty years later.

C This pond is known as the 'Keeper's Pond' after the Keeper's Cottage which used to stand nearby. The keeper was here to manage the grouse moors on the Blorenge, but the little stone cottage was demolished around 1970. The pond is also called Pen-ffordd-goch Pond, meaning 'Head of the red road'. When constructed in 1828, however, it was known as 'The Forge Pond'. It occupies about 2 acres (0.8 hectares) and was built as a header pond to supply Garnddyrys Forge, below.

Walk 27
YSGYRYD FAWR
2.5 miles (4 km) Moderate

This is a rewarding walk along the ridge of Gwent's Holy Mountain. Ysgyryd Fawr's isolated position enhances the views from its 1595 ft (486 m) summit, with the Black Mountains to the north-west, Herefordshire to the east and the Usk flowing into the Bristol Channel to the south. The open hill, above the perimeter fence, is National Trust property. This route gives you an easy mountain climb.

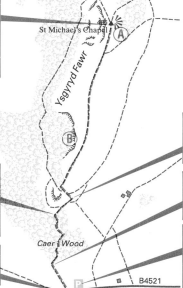

6 *Retrace your steps, enjoying the view from the opposite direction, with the Sugar Loaf now on your right. Notice the steep cliffs where a massive landslip left a deep cutting on the western (Sugar Loaf) side.*

5 *Climb up to the ridge, with its fine view of the Sugar Loaf on your left. Carry on along the ridge to the 'trig.' point.*

4 *Cross the stone stile in the wall ahead. Turn right along the perimeter path for 50 yds (45 m) before turning left from it up the right side of a picturesque dingle to reach the open hillside.*

3 *Cross a stile and bear right along a waymarked path through the wood. The path veers left as it climbs.*

2 *Cross the stile in the roadside hedge and follow the fenced path across the field to the wood ahead.*

1 *Park your car in the small, signposted car park on the left side of the B4521 about 3 miles (4.8 km) north-east of Abergavenny. Walk back down the road for 50 yds (45 m) to a public footpath signpost on your right.*

A Near the cracked and jagged summit of Ysgyryd Fawr (The Skirrid in English) is a hollow in the ground that marks the site of a chapel dedicated to St Michael the Archangel, who is supposed to have appeared here once. Ysgyryd Fawr has long been a holy mountain, with its soil in demand for sprinkling on coffins at burials. Here it was, during the days of persecution, that the Roman Catholics of Gwent (which remained the most Roman Catholic part of Wales after the Reformation) celebrated their Masses. In 1676 Pope Clement X promised plenary indulgences to those who went up on the feast day of St Michael. This provoked a fierce local Protestant backlash.

B The steep cliffs on the western side of Ysgyryd Fawr are attributed by geologists to an earthquake, which is traditionally dated to the moment of Christ's death. Another legend claims the massive landslip which left the chasm was caused by a leap of Siôn Cent, the mysterious local wizard who was at least a contemporary of Owain Glynŵr in the early 15th century, if not the fugitive freedom fighter's 'alter ego'. Noah's Ark has also been blamed for scraping the mountain.

Walk 28
RAMSEY SOUND
6 miles (9.6 km) Moderate

0   1 mile

0   1 km

This is as fine a coastal walk as you are likely to find anywhere. The path is good and clear, following the low but sheer cliffs, and the coast is indented with small bays, with several little islands offshore.

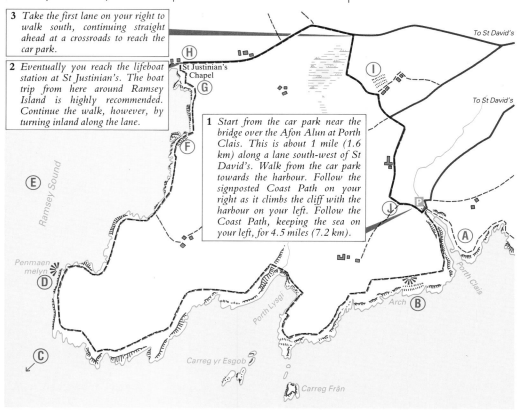

3 *Take the first lane on your right to walk south, continuing straight ahead at a crossroads to reach the car park.*

2 *Eventually you reach the lifeboat station at St Justinian's. The boat trip from here around Ramsey Island is highly recommended. Continue the walk, however, by turning inland along the lane.*

1 *Start from the car park near the bridge over the Afon Alun at Porth Clais. This is about 1 mile (1.6 km) along a lane south-west of St David's. Walk from the car park towards the harbour. Follow the signposted Coast Path on your right as it climbs the cliff with the harbour on your left. Follow the Coast Path, keeping the sea on your left, for 4.5 miles (7.2 km).*

A Afon Alun flows into the sea at Porth Clais, the harbour for St David's.

B There is a good view from here to the Island of Skomer.

C Ynys Bery.

D The ruins of a copper mine.

E Ramsey Island, or Ynys Dewi.

F Castell Heinif, an Iron Age fort.

G You can join a boat trip around Ramsey Island at St Justinian's lifeboat station.

H The ruins of St Justinian's Chapel mark the saint's burial place.

I Clegyr-Boia was a hill-fort occupied by Boia, an Irish chief.

J St David was baptised at this well.

Walk 29
SYMOND'S YAT
2 miles (3.2 km) Moderate

```
0                                    1 mile
├───┼───┼───┼───┼───┼───┼───┼───┤
0                      1 km
```

Symonds Yat is the most popular place for sightseers and walkers in the Wye Valley. They are well catered for, with ample parking at the Yat Rock car park and a choice of places offering refreshments and accommodation, while a ferryman still pulls a flat bottomed boat across the river by a rope. The Wye makes a 5 mile (8 km) bend here, but the isthmus is only 500 yards (450 m) across.

4 *Descend to the river, passing a ruined house. Walk along the Wye Valley Walk, with the river on your left and past a cottage on your right.*

3 *Turn right down a field to the lane. Turn left up the lane for 20 yards (18 m) to a signpost on your right. Bear right up through the trees to a road. Turn left up this road for 50 yards (45 m) to a signpost on your right. Bear right along this path to reach a forest track. Look for 'pudding stone' rocks on your right just as the track bends right. Turn left here down the waymarked path.*

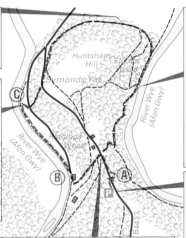

5 *Follow the well-trodden path into the trees on your right, where it is waymarked. Pass a ruin on your right and climb up to a signpost at the side of a forest track. Cross this track to climb the steps opposite to reach another signpost. Leave the Wye Valley Walk here by turning right towards Yat Rock. The path soon bends left uphill. Pass a ruined cottage on your left and bend right at Rosary Cottage, then left to the road at a signpost. Turn left up this road to the car park.*

1 *Park in the car park near Symond's Yat Rock (small fee). This is at the end of the B4432, 4 miles (6.4 km) north of Coleford, which is 5 miles (8 km) east of Monmouth. Walk past the refreshments kiosk to cross the road by the footbridge. Turn left for a fine view of the River Wye from 504 ft (153 m) at Symond's Yat Rock. Return to the footbridge, descend to the road and walk along it under the footbridge.*

2 *Opposite the stone arches of two old lime kilns, turn left down a signposted path to the riverside. Emerge by the Royal Hotel, where you turn right along the waymarked Wye Valley Walk. Pass the ferry at the Saracen's Head. Follow the yellow arrows to walk with the river on your left and a caravan site on your right. Keep along the riverbank until another ferry (which goes to Ye Olde Ferrie Inne).*

A Symonds Yat Rock offers unrivalled views over the Wye Valley. Here you will see what is termed an 'incised meander' by the river. Symonds was a High Sherriff of Herefordshire in the 17th century, while yat is an old English word for gate or pass. This is an extremely popular place, especially with bird-watchers (peregrine falcons can be seen here). The original peregrines abandoned this site in the early 1950's, when the growing use of pesticides took their toll. New birds settled in 1982 and are being watched over by the RSPB.

B The chain ferry at the Saracen's Head is a king's charter ferry dating back to at least the 17th century. Both this and **C** the ferry at Ye Olde Ferrie Inne operate during the day throughout the year, unless weather conditions are too bad. You can also take a river cruise from here.

PENMAEN DEWI (ST DAVID'S HEAD)

3.8 miles (6.1 km) Moderate

```
0                                          1 mile
├────┬────┬────┬────┬────┬────┬────┬────┬────┤
0                          1 km
```

St David's Head is one of Wales' most famous headlands, a prominent feature of a coastline that was busy in the days when communication depended largely on the sea. The route from southern Britain to Ireland intersected the great sea route along the west coast of Europe here.

4 Pass a second notice about climbing restrictions on your left. Shortly after this, turn right, away from the Coast Path. Bear right along this track, with the peak of Carn Llidi ahead on your left and Ramsey Island across the sea ahead on your right. Shortly after another track joins yours, turn left across a stream. The path veers left uphill.

5 Keep to the uphill path to join a wall on your right. Walk beside this wall, with a fine view of Whitesand Bay below on your right. When you come to a junction with a concrete path, turn sharply left uphill to reach the concrete platform of an old military installation on Carn Llidi Bychan. Follow a rough path to Carn Llidi.

6 Retrace your steps to Carn Llidi Bychan and follow the concrete path downhill back to the track beside the wall on your right. Continue past a signposted access path to the youth hostel on your left and go over a stile beside a gate to go through Upper Porthmawr farmyard. Continue along a hedged track, bearing right, then left along a metalled lane to the road, where you turn right to reach the car park at Whitesand Bay.

3 Turn sharply right at St David's Head to walk with the sea still on your left. Pause at the second inlet (Ogof Coetan), where a notice warns of climbing restrictions on the cliffs. Turn right here to walk to the ancient burial chamber, Coetan Arthur. Return to the Coast Path, which keeps behind the cliffs.

2 Follow the Coast Path, crossing a footbridge and bearing left.

1 Park your car at Whitesand Bay (fee). This is at the end of the B4583, 2 miles (3.2 km) northwest of St David's. As you face the sea at the car park entrance, turn right along the signposted Coast Path. After 20 yds (18 m) you will pass the site of St Patrick's Chapel on your left. Keep to the fenced path, ignoring stiles leading to the rocky promontory (Trwynhwrddyn or the Ram's Nose) on your left. Cross a stile ahead into National Trust land - Penmaen Dewi.

A Whitesand Bay is a fine, west-facing beach. Its sands cover the remains of a prehistoric forest and the Roman station of Menapia.

B A concrete slab in the field on your left marks the site of an old chapel, the spot from where St Patrick set sail to Ireland.

C Porthmelgan is a small, sheltered beach. The valley leading to it was cultivated in ancient times.

D Notice a great stone rampart, known as Clawdd y Milwyr or Warrior's Dyke.

E Penmaen Dewi or St David's Head was known as the Promontory of the Eight Perils (Octopitarum Promontarium) by the Romans, referring to the eight reefs and islets now known as the Bishops and Clerks.

F Coetan Arthur is a Stone Age burial chamber which may date back to 3000 BC.

Walk 31
MAENORBYR (MANORBIER)
2 miles (3.2 km) Easy

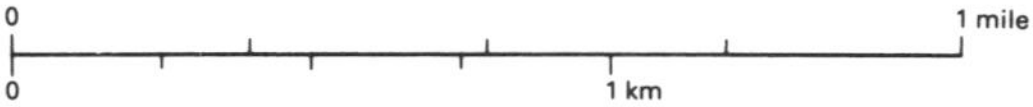

This is a trail around the various historical sites of Manorbier, the village made famous by Giraldus Cambrensis, who was born here in 1146. The place name is pronounced Manor-beer, and was called simply Beere in the 14th century, although it was probably originally known as Maenor Pyr - Pyr's manor. The Pembrokeshire Coast Path is followed back from King's Quoit. *Take care on this cliff-edge path.*

1 *Park your car in the National Park car park (fee) below the castle, to the south of Manorbier, which is on the B4585, off the A4139 about 5 miles (8 km) west of Tenby, from where there are also train and bus services. From the car park entrance, turn left along the road for 20 yds (18 m), then turn right up a gated lane. Pass the ruins of an old mill on your left. Continue along the lane and when you reach a water works go through a small gate on your right. Cross a stile on your left to reach a round building (the castle dovecote).*

2 *Retrace your steps to the car park entrance but continue to Manorbier castle's side entrance, on your left. Visit the castle and return to this side entrance.*

3 *Turn left up the road for 100 yds (90 m), then turn right along the lane to the church.*

4 *Go ahead through the gate to the churchyard, with the church on your left and its car park on your right. At the top, turn right along the distinct path to a stile ahead.*

5 *Walk around the right hand edge of this field.*

6 *Bear right along the path through the heathland. TAKE CARE when crossing the fissure, the depth of which may be obscured by vegetation. Look for the large capstone of King's Quoit, a Stone Age burial chamber down on your right. Follow the path through the bracken to it.*

7 *Turn right along the Coast Path to the beach. Follow the track inland back to the car park.*

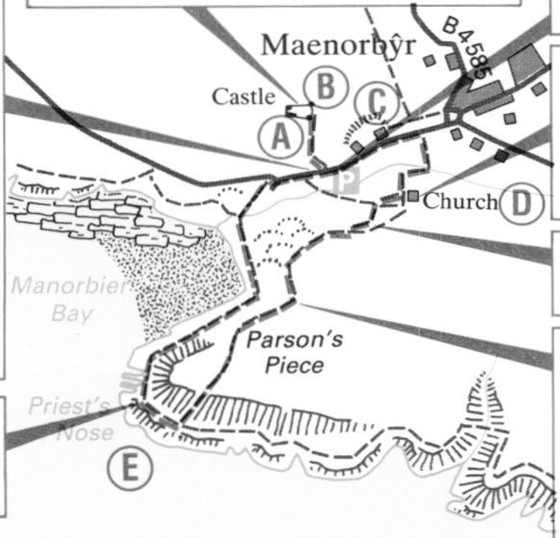

(map labels: Maenorbyr, Castle, B4585, B, C, A, P, Church D, Manorbier Bay, Parson's Piece, Priest's Nose, E)

A This ruined mill served Manorbier from Norman times until the 19th century. The waterwheel has gone but the wheel shaft remains, while pieces of millstone lie on the floor. The miller's cottage, back at the car park entrance, has been converted into a toilet block.

B The dovecote, or pigeon-house, is a typically Norman structure. Go inside to see the nesting holes. Birds were a good source of fresh food during the winter, when lack of winter feed made meat scarce.

C Gerald also described how the castle at Manorbier, where he was born into the Norman de Barri family (but with a mother of Welsh descent), was well defended by turrets and bulwarks. These would probably have been made of wood in the 12th century but the stone walls erected in the 13th century remain. Manorbier's relatively peaceful history has preserved the castle well and it is worth the admission fee just to see the wax effigies of chained prisoners in the stinking dungeon.

D Manorbier church's imposing tower used to stand apart from the building. Giraldus Cambrensis once sought sanctuary here during a Welsh attack, although its earliest remaining feature is a 14th century oak loft.

E People lived here long before the Normans. The King's Quoit is a Neolithic burial chamber (about 5000 years old). The pillars which support the capstone have collapsed.

Walk 32
ST NON'S CHAPEL & WELL
4 miles (6.4 km) Easy

0						1 mile

0			1 km	

This is a varied walk along country lanes to a most interesting section of the Pembrokeshire Coast Path, then back to the city of St David's.

Although the walking is easy, care is needed both with tourist traffic on the country lanes and, especially, with children along the

Coast Path, where the footpath can be both *spectacularly and dangerously close to the edge of the cliff.*

3 *Do not cross the bridge over the River Alun at Porth Clais, but bear right along the lane to St David's. Bear left down towards St David's Cathedral, crossing the road to St Justinian's. Visit the cathedral and the remains of the Bishop's Palace. Walk up to the fortified gateway of Porth y Twr and on to the old Cross Square.*

4 *Continue up the High Street to the Cocyn Round, a round white wall, where you fork right, back to the car park.*

1 *Park your car at the signposted car park between the A487 road to Haverfordwest and the minor road to Caerfai on the eastern edge of St David's, opposite the Grove Hotel. Walk down the signposted road to Caerfai, passing Caerfai farm. Walk down the path from the coastal car park to join the Pembrokeshire Coast Path.*

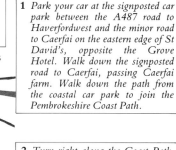

2 *Turn right along the Coast Path, with the sea on your left. After rounding the first headland, notice a building ahead on your right. This is a monastery built near the ruins of St Non's chapel. Fork right just before the monastery to walk past it and follow a path lined with Hydrangea shrubs to the holy well on your left, a statue of the Virgin Mary on your right and the ruins of the 6th century chapel through a gate ahead of you. Return to the Coast Path and follow it to Porth Clais Harbour, with its restored lime kilns.*

A Notice the distinctive Twr-y-felin across the field on your left. This is an old windmill, erected in 1806 to grind local corn.

B Caerfai boasts a sandy beach which is suitable for bathing (except at high tide). The sides of the bay afford views of impressive Cambrian rock formations some 500 million years old. Stone was quarried from here to build St David's cathedral.

C St Non was the mother of St David, who is said to have been born here in a thunderstorm in 462 AD. The ruined 6th century chapel marks the spot, while the nearby holy well is said to have sprung up in the same storm.

D Limekilns at Porth Clais harbour show that lime was landed here to be spread on local fields.

E Only the top of the cathedral

tower is visible as you approach St David's. The medieval cathedral was built on the site of St David's 6th century monastery, which was hidden in the valley for safety. Two pilgrimages to St David's used to count as the equivalent of one to Rome. The Bishop's Palace is also worth a visit.

F This 14th-century stepped cross is the focal point of the 'village city'.

Walk 33
BOSHERSTON LILY PONDS
2 miles (3.2 km) Easy

0   1 mile
0   1 km

June is the best month to do this walk, when the white water lilies are in bloom. The lily ponds are in the western arm of the Stackpole lakes, which cover some 80 acres (32 hectares) and constitute the largest area of fresh water in the Pembrokeshire Coast National Park.

1 *Start from the National Park car park near Bosherston church. This is signposted off the B4319 road about 4 miles (6.4 km) south of Pembroke. Follow the signposted path from the car park to the lily ponds.*

2 *At the National Trust cairn by the pond, turn left along the clear lakeside path, with the water on your right. Take care when going ahead across a narrow, railed, stone causeway to the opposite bank of this western arm of the pond.*

3 *Follow the lakeside path on your right. This cuts across a headland (behind which is an Iron Age fort), to a second stone causeway and bridge across the pond.*

Bosherston

Fort

4 *Walk along the clearly defined path around the next headland to a signpost. Ignore the sign pointing up the eastern arm of the pond (unless you wish to extend the walk by following this path as far as you can and then retracing your steps back to the signpost). Proceed in the direction of Broadhaven by crossing a third stone causeway.*

6 *Back at the National Trust cairn, retrace your steps to the car park. You could visit the church before leaving.*

5 *At the southern end of the pond, cross a narrow stream which flows into the sea. Turn right along the* signposted path back to Bosherston, with the pond on your right.

A This Iron Age fort was strategically sited in about 400 BC over what would have been an inlet of the sea. The steep slopes of its hill would have been enhanced by ditches and ramparts. These can only be viewed from below, however, as there is no access to the site.

B These ponds were artificially created in the 18th century when the Stackpole Estate had passed by marriage to the Cawdor Estate of Scotland. 6000 acres (2400 hectares) of the original estate were taken over by the Army at the start of the second world war and now form the Castlemartin Army Range, which the West German Army use extensively for training. The Cawdor family transferred 2000 acres (800 hectares) to the National Trust in 1976 and the rest to a national pensions fund in 1977. The pond water is rich in lime and fed by underwater springs. The rich marl bed encourages the growth of underwater plants, which in turn support plenty of fish and bird life. The water lilies covering the surface and the stonewort carpeting the bottom of the western arm indicate the lack of pollution. In contrast, other arms have been enriched by local sewerage. Coots feed upon the stonewort, while pike feed upon roach. The Emperor Dragonfly and the Blue Damselfly can also be seen.

C A wall was built here to create the lily ponds.

D Bosherston church is dedicated to St Michael, suggesting an ancient site. St Govan, the local saint who may have been King Arthur's Sir Gawain, is depicted in the transept windows.

Walk 34
CAERIW
2 miles (3.2 km) Easy

0 ———————————————————— 1 mile

0 ———————————————————— 1 km

This is a gentle, waymarked walk in a very picturesque and interesting part of Wales. Please note, however, that both Carew Castle and the French Mill may be closed on Saturdays. The setting is the Daugleddau, where tidal waterways are exposed as muddy pills or creeks, attracting many birds at low tide. The area is known as the 'inner sanctuary' of the Pembrokeshire Coast National Park.

3 *Ignore the stile on your right, but turn left across the footbridge and walk along the dam to visit the French Mill.*

4 *Bear left up the lane and turn sharply right up a track until a public footpath signpost directs you over a stone step on your left.*

5 *Walk with the hedge on your left to a stile ahead. Cross it and pass a disused quarry on your right before turning left over a signposted stone step. Turn right immediately to walk with the hedge on your right to a signposted stile ahead.*

6 *Turn right to cross the old bridge into Milton. Bear left up to the A477, which you cross carefully to the lane opposite. Walk up to the first turning on your left.*

2 *Turn left along a lane to a picnic site. Continue along the footpath with the Mill Pond on your left.*

1 *Start at the National Park car park opposite the war memorial at Carew. This is on the A4075, half a mile (0.8 km) from its junction with the A477, about 4 miles (6.4 km) east of Pembroke. Turn right out of the car park and cross the road to see the Carew Cross on your left. Next, visit the castle. A combined ticket can be bought to include the French Mill. Continue across the bridge.*

8 *Visit St Mary's church, then turn right from its entrance to follow the road back to the A477. Cross this road carefully to walk along the A4075 back to the car park.*

7 *Follow the track on your left, which bears right after a farm. Continue to walk beside a stream on your left to reach Carew Cheriton church.*

A Carew Cross was erected in 1035 in memory of Maredudd ap Edwin, a descendant of the great law-maker Hywel Dda (Howell the Good). It is a fine example of an early Christian monument, standing an imposing 14 ft (4.2 m) high. It is basically Celtic, with geometric patterns decorating it. There is a Viking influence, however, reflecting their settlement which helped establish the Landsker, the invisible line between north and south Pembrokeshire. In the Middle Ages this was part of 'Little England beyond Wales'. The inscription on the cross is in Latin: 'Margitent Rex etg (uin) filius' (King Mariteut Son of Edwin).

B Carew Castle occupies a good defensive position overlooking a tidal creek. This land formed part of Nest's dowry when the beautiful daughter of Rhys ap Twdr, Prince of Dyfed, was married to Gerald de Windsor, Constable of Pembroke, in 1100. Gerald started building a stone castle here and his descendants took the name de Carew from it. Its most famous event was the Great Tournament of 1507, probably the last of its kind in Britain.

C The French Mill is so-named because its millstones came from France. It is the only surviving tidal mill, using stored tidal water from its mill pond to drive its wheels on the ebb (falling) tide. Grinding local corn, such a mill was first recorded here in 1541.

D Limestone used to be quarried here and transported by canal barge to Radford Pill.

E St Mary's church, Carew Cheriton.

56

RHOSILI (RHOSSILI)

4.3 miles (6.9 km) Easy

0   1 mile
0   1 km

Save this walk for a fine day as it would be a shame to miss the splendid views, which extend across the whole of the Gower Peninsula to the east, to the old counties of Pembrokeshire and Carmarthenshire (now Dyfed) in the north, across the sea to Devon and Somerset in the south and to Lundy Island in the south-west. After enjoying the heights of Rhosili Down, the return is along the sands of Rhossili Bay, where the timbers of an old wreck can be seen at low tide. You then regain the heights of the present village of Rhosili by passing the ancient village site.

A Rhosili parish church was probably built in the 14th century by Anglo-Norman settlers. Look for the memorial to Petty Officer Edgar Evans on the north wall of the nave. He reached the South Pole with Captain Scott in 1912 before freezing to death.

B The Beacon is the highest point on the Gower at 632 ft (193 m).

C Sweyne's houses are probably very old burial tombs. Their name is derived from Sweyne, however, who was a Danish Viking chief. He gave his name to Swansea and may have been buried here

D The solitary building facing the sea is the Old Parsonage, or Rectory. It was built here as the rector used to serve both the parishes of Rhosili and Llangennith. It is reputedly haunted.

E The 'Helvetia' was wrecked here in November 1887. Her 500 tons of cargo was timber and she was made of oak, so she drifted here after being abandoned by her crew. Her deck-boards now floor a local kitchen - most of the old farms here are built of wreckwood.

F The site of the old village.

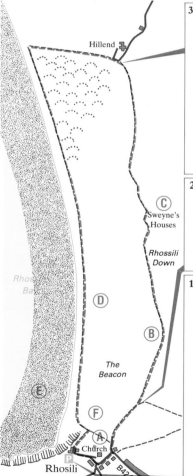

3 Turn left through the caravan site to reach the beach, where you turn left to walk along the foreshore back towards Rhosili. If your walk happens to coincide with low tide you can inspect the remains of the wreck of the Helvetia. Near the wreck, turn left to climb the steps inland. You pass the site of the ancient village of Rhosili, which seems to have been totally engulfed by wind blown sand during the early 14th century. The steps eventually lead you back to modern Rhosili with its car park.

2 Follow the crest of Rhosili Down, passing the Beacon on your left and Sweyne's houses or tombs about half a mile (0.8 km) further on. Descend to Hillend camping and caravanning site, which is at the end of a lane leading to Llangennith.

1 Park at the car park (fee) at the end of the B4247 at Rhosili. This is at the south-west corner of the Gower Peninsula about 19 miles (30.4 km) west of Swansea, from where there is a bus service (18). Turn right inland along the road from the car park and take the path on your left to Rhosili's parish church, dedicated to St Mary the Virgin. After visiting this, continue through the churchyard and bear left along a track past farm buildings on your right and ignoring a signposted path down to the beach on your left. Go ahead through a gate to follow a distinct path uphill.

Walk 36
PORT EINON (PORT EYNON)
2.8 miles (4.5 km) Easy

Gower was the first place in Great Britain to be designated as an Area of Outstanding Natural Beauty, and this walk shows you why. It goes through a nature reserve to reach a fine stretch of coastline, complete with raised beaches, caves, a horse-shoe bay and cliffs.

1 *Park at the car park (fee) near the beach at Port Eynon, which is at the end of the A4118 about 15 miles (24 km) west of Swansea, from where there is a bus service (18). Walk back up the road inland, bearing left at St Cattwg's church. Turn left along the signposted road to Overton. Pass the Boarlands on your left to reach the green.*

2 *Walk past the village green on your right and ignore a signposted footpath on your left to continue ahead along a lane which deteriorates to a bridleway. Go through the gate marked 'Nature Reserve' and turn left along a path descending into the valley. Cross a stile in the wall on your left, near old lime kilns.*

5 *Walk inland, towards Port Einion, from the memorial stone. Port Eynon Bay is on your right and you can overlook the site of the Salthouse (which was being excavated in 1988). Bear right to drop down to where a path leads to the old lifeboat station, which is now a youth hostel. Turn left over a stile at the side of the youth hostel to walk back to the car park.*

4 *Cross a stile and, ignoring a path which leads inland, continue around the horseshoe bay of Overton Mere to Culver Hole cave. Be VERY careful when scrambling down the rocks for a better view, and avoid high tide. Retrace your steps over the rocks to follow the path up to the top of the cliff, where there is a stone erected by the Gower Society in memory of Gwent Jones and Stephen Lee.*

3 *Follow the clear coastal path, with the sea on your right. Notice a small cave in the cliff on your left. This is Willbower.*

Port Einion

Overton

Overton Cliff

Porth Eynon Bay

The Salt House

Culver Hole

Monument

A Willbower is just one of several caves in this stretch of coast. The most famous cave is Paviland Cave, a mile to the west of here, where a headless human skeleton was found in 1823. Recent radiocarbon tests date this to about 18,000 years ago. **Don't be tempted to explore this cave, however, as several people have died trying to reach it.**

B Among the many shipwrecks along this coast is that of the 'Rene', which foundered on 8th January, 1886, on the Overton cliffs. This Breton barque was bound from Cardiff for France with 450 tons of coal.

C Culver Hole Cave is walled up and makes an impregnable stronghold. King Einion is said to have resorted to it after losing the rest of his land to the English. It was later a smuggler's retreat and a pigeon house.

D The site of the Salthouse mansion.

E Port Eynon's old lifeboat station.

Walk 37
AFAN ARGOED
3 miles (4.8 km) Easy

Afan Argoed Country Park is known locally as 'Little Switzerland'. It scenic beauty is made easily accessible by waymarked forest walks. This one follows Afon Afan before returning along the bed of a dismantled railway. The story of the Afan valley is told in the Welsh Miners' Museum, which received the Prince of Wales Award for 1976, near the start of this walk.

4 *Bear left downhill along the path that is waymarked in orange. Bear right when this joins the lower parallel track. Then continue around a sharp left turn to the river. Cross the footbridge and retrace your steps to the car park, making sure you visit the Welsh Miners Museum before leaving.*

3 *When you reach the bed of the old railway, turn left along it to follow the river downstream but from a higher level. Go right when you reach a fork. This takes you to an old tunnel entrance.*

2 *Cross the bridge and turn right to follow the river upstream. Keep to this track for 1 mile (1.6 km) until an orange waymarked path climbs up through the trees on your left, near a picnic site.*

1 *Start from the car park at the Countryside Centre, Afan Argoed Country Park. This is 6 miles (9.6 km) north-east of Port Talbot on the A4l07 (M4 junction 40) and is easily reached by bus from Port Talbot (no 232). Walk past the Welsh Miners Museum on your left to follow the walk waymarked in orange. Walk with the main road on your right to an underpass, where you turn right and descend to the footbridge over the river.*

Map: Cwm Afan, Dismantled Railway, Afon Afan, A4107, Cynonville, Afon Argoed Country Park

A Afan Argoed is part of industrial South Wales which has been made into a popular country park. This area was criss-crossed by railways and dominated by coal-mining in the 19th century. The natural beauty of these hills and valleys had already been affected by the destruction of the native broad-leaved forests to provide timber for shipbuilding and making charcoal for iron smelting. Iron was made more cheaply from about 1750, however, when coke made from coal replaced charcoal. South Wales had abundant supplies of both iron ore and coal. These resources were fully exploited, transforming the landscape in the process and gravely affecting the ecology. By the late 19th century the iron industries were replaced by steel making near the coast, using imported iron ore. Coal was the major export, with steam power being applied universally. The end of the First World War saw competition from abroad, demands for better pay and working conditions at home and technical problems with deeper mining. The 1926 General Strike was followed by the depression of the 1930s. When the coal industry was nationalised in 1947, massive capital investment was required after years of neglect. This led to the closure of many uneconomic pits, while nuclear power, oil and gas caused further pit closures in the 1960s. Coal-mining ended in this region in 1970. By 1976, the Welsh Miners Museum was established at Afan Argoed. It is open daily from April to October (10.30am-6pm) and at weekends in the winter (10.30am-5pm).

B This is the trackbed of the old South Wales Mineral Railway.

C Cyfylchi Tunnel was 1109 yards long and was built between 1856 and 1863. The discovery of large structural faults in 1947 caused its closure.

Walk 38
CAS-GWENT (CHEPSTOW)
4 miles (6.4 km) Moderate

This delightful walk takes you from a fine example of medieval castle building across the River Wye from Wales to England, where you pick up Offa's Dyke Path. This is followed through the trees between the Wye and the cliffs of Wintour's Leap. The river-bank is then followed for a while before turning to ascend and gain a fine view from the cliff tops on the way back to Chepstow.

A Chepstow Castle is perched on limestone cliffs above the Wye. There is a cave in the cliff below it which was once entered by a potter named Thompson, who claimed to have seen King Arthur and his sleeping knights there. The castle was built in successive stages and illustrates the story of castle building from the Normans right up to the re-modelling of its defences after the Civil War. William FitzOsbern secured this strategic site for the victor of the Battle of Hastings within a decade of 1066. His stone keep was strengthened by a curtain wall and flanking towers with arrow slits by the Earl of Pembroke in about 1200. A strongly defended barbican was then built at the upper end. A large hall block was added in Edward I's reign. Probably the best known occupier was Earl Richard de Clare, the 'Strongbow' who conquered Leinster (in Ireland) and who died in 1176. The castle has housed many prisoners, including Henry Marten, who signed the death warrant of Charles I. Dr Orville Owen, an American who believed Francis Bacon was the real author of Shakespeare's plays, had this area searched for missing manuscripts in the early 1900s. His digging exposed a Roman bridge.

B The old stone tower was probably a 16th century watch-tower or beacon.

C St James' church, Lancant, was closed in the mid 19th century. Lepers were buried just to the west of here.

D The cliffs above the Wye at this point have been quarried, which is a pity as this is supposed to be the site of Wintour's Leap. Sir John Wintour was a stalwart Royalist in the Civil War (not without self-interest as Charles I leased the whole of the Forest of Dean to him, and he employed 500 axemen to fell its trees). During an escape from Cromwell's troops, Wintour lept his horse over the 200 ft (60 m) cliff now called after him. In fact, Wintour's famous escape was probably on October 14th, 1644, when he scrambled down Sedbury Cliff above the River Severn, not the Wye, and on foot, to escape by a small boat.

E Tutshill is the name of the place on the Gloucestershire bank of the River Wye, opposite Chepstow. It is an example of a place named after the Egyptian God Thoth. Alfred Watkins, the pioneer ley-hunter who wrote *The Old Straight Track* in 1925, realised this after coming across so many sighting-mounds called Toot, Tot, Tut or similar, all derived from the Welsh word twt, meaning mound. Such mounds are mark-points on track-ways (or, according to more recent ley-hunters, on earth-energy lines). As such they are linked with Thoth, who was, like Hermes or Mercury, responsible for pathways. As it happens the old Roman road from Venta Silurum (Caerwent) to Glevum (Glouces-ter) went through Tutshill. The Silures were the greatest tribe of Ancient Britain, able to withstand the invading Romans under their leader Caradoc (Caractacus) for years. The Romans respected them and the royal house of the Silures married Roman nobility. The Silures also received the very earliest Christians, the band that reached Britain with Joseph of Arimathea and became the new religion's first converts. The link with the east was real and the Celtic god Tout was Romanised to Toutates and treated as the equiva-lent of Mercury – and Thoth.

F Just before you return to the car park, visit the museum on your left. Chepstow is an English name, meaning 'market place'.

0 _____ 1 mile
0 _____ 1 km

3 *Keep right when you join another path near an old lime kiln. Continue to a metalled lane where you keep right to reach the B4228 road.*

2 *Reach the river bank where the river bends. Keep close to the river, on your left, until you cross a tubular metal stile. Pass the ruins of St James' church, Lancaut, on your right and turn right, uphill, as directed by a yellow arrow. Bear right up a waymarked path, over another tubular metal stile and through trees.*

4 *Turn right along this road, stopping to admire the view from Wintour's Leap at the sharp bend on your right.*

5 *Turn right at the Nature Reserve just before the first house on your right. Take GREAT care, especially with children, at the cliff top. Turn left, with the Wye below you on the right. The path soon leaves the cliff edge to run beside the backs of houses on your left, Go ahead across the end of a cul-de-sac and eventually reach the road at an arch.*

6 *Turn right along the road for 200 yds (180 m) to a waymarked Offa's Dyke Path kissing-gate on your right. Walk along this path, with the wall on your right, until you reach a stile on your left.*

7 *You crossed this stile on the way out, so it is easy to retrace your steps along the waymarked Offa's Dyke Path and down to the bridge back to Chepstow Castle. This peaceful footpath route is preferable to completing a circle by following roads. You can gain a fresh view of a path by walking it in the reverse direction, and can relax from route-finding.*

(Map labels: St James's Church, C, Wintour's Leap, D, Woodcroft, Afon Gwy (River Wye), Offa's Dyke, B, B4228, E, A48, Cas-Gwent (Chepstow), P, A, A48)

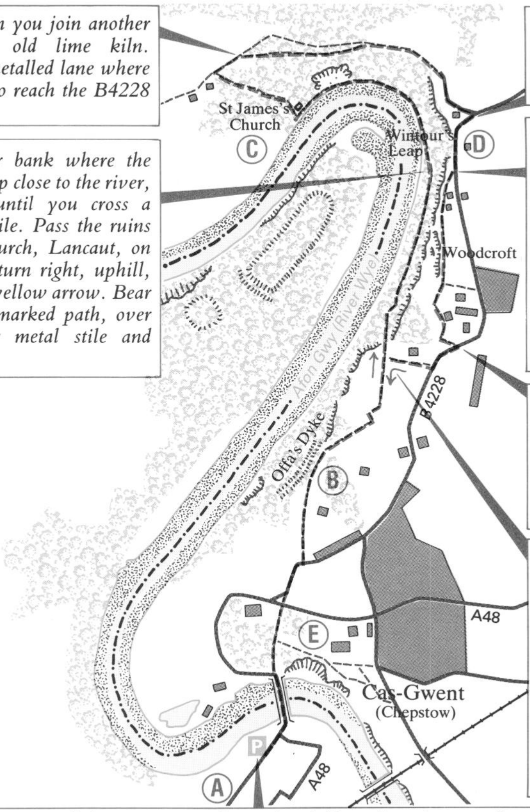

1 *Chepstow is easy to reach by train or bus and is the first turning off the M4 as you enter Wales across the Severn Road Bridge. Park your car near the entrance to Chepstow castle, which is well signposted at the northern end of the town. After visiting the castle, walk down the road to cross the River Wye by the narrow iron road bridge which connects Wales to England. Go straight ahead up the lane for pedestrians, which is soon joined by the waymarked Offa's Dyke Path.*

Cross the A48 road at the top of the lane and follow the minor road ahead for 150 yds (135 m) to a waymarked stile on your left just before the first house. Follow the well-defined path, which is part of Offa's Dyke Path, along the right-hand edge of this field. Pass an old round tower on your right, continue to the far corner of the field and turn right over a waymarked stile to walk with the wall on your left to a stile, which you cross. Walk down a short passage and turn right along a

drive for 40 yds (36 m) to a stile on your left. Cross it and follow the clear path to a stile where you depart from Offa's Dyke Path by turning left. Walk under a small bridge with a wall on your right into trees. Follow the distinct path which descends very gradually through the trees, with the River Wye on your left and the quarried cliffs of Wintour's Leap on your right.

61

Walk 39
TYNDYRN (TINTERN)
5 miles (8 km) Easy

It was near Tintern that Wordsworth immortalised the Wye valley in verse. 'O sylvan Wye! Thou wanderer through the woods. How often has my spirit turned to thee!' The great poet was just one visitor here in the Wye valley's romantic period.

It wasn't only Wordsworth who found 'the power of joy' so that he could 'see into the life of things' here. The Cistercians chose to cut down the dense forest and build an abbey here in 1131, then rebuild it on a grander scale 150 years later. This walk is well waymarked, as befits a route that goes from one long distance path, the Wye Valley Walk, to another, Offa's Dyke Path. The Dyke is followed on this walk for about 2 miles (3.2 km), providing glimpses of the Wye from its tree-clad height.

A The picturesque ruins of Tintern Abbey have long been a tourist attraction. But it is the walker arriving via Offa's Dyke Path or the Wye Valley Walk who will experience the greatest sense of pilgrimage. This was a Cistercian monastery, founded by Walter fitz Richard, the Norman Lord of Chepstow, in 1131. Monks continued to live here until the Dissolution of the Monasteries by Henry VIII in 1536. The Cistercians originated in France and were noted for their simple living and asceticism. This included living in isolated places and emphasising manual labour. Most of the heavy agricultural labour was undertaken by lay brothers, who lived at the abbey as part of the full community but were bound by less severe rules than the choir monks. Lavish gifts eventually corrupted the original simplicity, while the Black Death (1348-49) led to a decline in the number of lay brothers and abbey estates were leased out to tenants. By 1536, Tintern was the wealthiest abbey in Wales. After the Dissolution, the buildings were robbed of their lead and stone. By 1800, the abbey ruins were a busy tourist attraction.

B The footbridge over the River Wye used to carry a tramway between the Wye Valley Railway and the wireworks at Tintern. The influence of the Cistercians led to iron being produced here from the 13th century. Britain's first water-powered wire-drawing mill was established here in 1566 and the first brass made in Britain also came from here. The water-mill between the road and the river was probably used to strip bark for tanning. Despite the new bridge and tramway (opened in 1876), the wireworks closed down in 1880).

C Your path is now over the mouth of a tunnel for the Wye Valley Railway. Opened in 1876, this line ran between Chepstow and Monmouth. Sadly, it closed in 1964.

D Offa's Dyke was built in the late 8th century by Offa, King of Mercia, to mark the boundary between his English kingdom and the Welsh. A 168 mile (269 km) long distance path now follows it from Chepstow to Prestatyn. It is a well-waymarked route. Such an agreed border was long overdue as the Saxons fought the Britons here in 509 A.D. The Britons won, but their elderly king, Tewdrig, was mortally wounded. Tewdrig had retired here, and gave his name to the place (Din Teyryn, meaning 'Fort of the Monarch', was corrupted to Tintern). Tewdrig was the father of Meurig and the grandfather of the great Arthur.

E The Devil's Pulpit is a limestone pillar where, according to legend, the Devil preached to the monks of Tintern. When he appeared in the abbey itself, however, he was doused in holy water and fled.

F The waymarked Wye Valley Walk follows the river valley for 52 miles (83.2 km) between Chepstow and Hereford. It continues in Powys.

Walk 39
TYNDYRN (TINTERN)
Continued

0   1 mile

0   1 km

[Map showing the walking route around Tyndyrn (Tintern), with labels: A466, Brockweir, River Wye (Afon Gwy), Caswell Wood, Tintern Parva, Tyndyrn (Tintern), Tintern Abbey, Passage Grove, Offa's Dyke, Devil's Pulpit, and markers B, C, D, E, F, P, A.]

2 Turn right when you reach a signpost pointing to the Devil's Pulpit. Walk up a track with the hedge on your right, following the Offa's Dyke Path waymarks. Bear right from a signpost along a hedged track to a stile beside a gate. Turn right across this and veer left uphill to Offa's Dyke, which is covered by trees.

3 Turn right along the Dyke, following the waymarked path. Cross a stile into the Fidenham section of Offa's Dyke. Continue along the waymarked path, across a track. When you reach a signpost take note of it for your return journey, but continue past it. After nearly half a mile (0.8 km) a sharp right turn in the path brings you to the Devil's Pulpit, which is a pillar of limestone just below the path overlooking the Wye Valley on your right.

4 Retrace your steps along Offa's Dyke to the signpost you passed nearly half-a-mile (0.8 km) before the Devil's Pulpit. Turn left here downhill to Tintern. Follow the yellow arrows right, then left, at a cross-path to continue down through the trees, bearing left. Bear right when you reach a path at a waymark post, then bear left with the main track to reach your outward path again. Keep left along it for Tintern.

1 Start from Tintern Abbey, where there is a car park and a bus stop. Tintern is on the A466 5 miles (8 km) north of Chepstow and on the no 69 bus route from Chepstow (the nearest railway station) to Monmouth. Follow the signposted path from the abbey entrance, with the River Wye on your right. Turn left to the main road, where you turn right for 100 yds (90 m), then turn right past a disused watermill to cross a footbridge. Bear right along the waymarked track for about 200 yds (180 m), then turn left up a steep, cobbled, waymarked path. Take the left-hand path where it forks and go ahead along the track, with the hedge on your left, to Brockweir.

Walk 40
CASTELL COCH
2 miles 93.2 km) Easy

0   1 mile
0   1 km

Castell Coch is one of the most picturesque buildings in Wales. It is a fairy-tale castle on the edge of Cardiff, accompanied by a wood which provides the citizens of Wales's capital city with a vital 'lung', the trees serving to muffle the noise of the nearby traffic.

2 *Join a track coming from your left at the top of the bank, where the trees change from broadleaved to evergreen. Bear right along this, ignoring narrow side-paths. Walk past a path on your right which is waymarked '7', but be prepared for waymarked path '6' on your right soon after it, when the barrier marking the entrance to this forest is not far ahead of you.*

1 *You can take the train to Taff's Well, or bus (no 26) to Tongwynlais to reach Castell Coch. Car drivers should follow the sign where Mill Road (which soon becomes Castle Road) leaves the Merthyr Road (A4054) in Tongwynlais, on the north-western edge of Cardiff. Start from the car park in front of the castle drawbridge. With the castle at your back, walk to the end of the car park, which is on your left, and climb up through the trees along the clear path on your left.*

3 *Turn right down this waymarked path '6'. Bear right at a fork uphill, passing '5' on your right and walking with evergreen trees on your right and broadleaved trees on your left.*

4 *Go ahead across a track and turn left at '13', where there is a 'T' junction. Continue past '24' on your right to a barrier (where signs point sharp left to a Countryside Centre).*

5 *Go ahead along the main path, bearing right to descend to the drive on your left where this meets the road at the entrance to the castle grounds. Turn right up the drive back to the castle.*

B

Heol-y-Fforest

FforestFawr

A

Drive

Castell Coch

Tongwynlais

A4054

Afon Taf

A Castell Coch is like a back-cloth for 'Sleeping Beauty'. Its name means Red Castle and it is not to be confused with Cardiff Castle, which is near the city centre. Both castles fell into the hands of the Marquess of Bute, however. The architect William Burges was employed to reconstruct the original 13th century castle, which had been built by Gilbert the Red, Earl of Gloucester, to protect the narrow gorge of the Taff from the Welsh. It was destroyed in the 15th century and left in ruins for centuries. An 18th century artist recorded a substantial corner tower and a legend tells of an impoverished lady living in it in 1780. She saw a ghost, supposedly of a former owner who had buried a chest of gold in an underground passage linking Castell Coch with Cardiff Castle during Cromwell's Civil War. He left two eagles to guard it. These eagles attacked a party who explored this passage and the gold hunters were glad to escape with their lives.

In 1871, however, Lord Bute cleared the site (exposing the red soil that gives the Castle its name) and had it extravagantly and imaginatively reconstructed. He could afford to do so as he was reputedly the richest man in the world, thriving on the family investments in the Cardiff area – the greatest coal port in the world. Lord Bute was a convert to Roman Catholicism and was interested in mysticism.

B This charming woodland walk forms part of the 'Cambrian Way' long distance path from Cardiff to Conwy.

64